LEAD
WELL

KIRSTEN MCKENNA

BLS, BPHED, Dip Positive Psychology

Contents

Acknowledgements

This voyage of self-discovery and extensive study would not have taken place without the support of my husband Paul, who encourages me every day to achieve more and truly develop my potential. Thank-you for believing in me and for being my biggest fan.

To my son Oban who fills my heart beyond measure and inspires me daily to laugh, play and savour each moment; you give me the courage when I need it most.

Thanks to my Mom for driving my love of learning through her emphasis on life-long education and whole-heartedly believing in me. To my Dad for teaching me the importance of effort, hard work, determination and resilience.

To all of the leaders who believed in me and let me fly, thank-you for the autonomy, for the ability to hone my craft, and for the honest feedback.

This book would not have been put together without the advice, support and persistent challenge offered by my mentor Mark Hodgson. Your insight, good humour and frankness have encouraged me every step of the way.

Introduction

We all possess the capacity to build our potential. No longer do scientists believe talent and capability are innate and fixed, instead these things are determined by *our own actions* to develop them.

When my parents told me to see what would happen if I applied myself, I took this as a personal challenge and put 110% into my second degree in education. Finishing top of my class with a 3.97gpa, I realised that they knew what they were talking about. My mother has always encouraged me in education and my father has always encouraged me to chase my dreams and because of their influence, I am consistently developing my potential.

> "We know what we are, but know not what we may be."
> *William Shakespeare*

Unfortunately, we typically neglect to apply ourselves whole-heartedly in all that we do. Many of us are not building our potential, rather we are maintaining the status quo, resting within our comfort zones where we feel safe and secure. Maintaining the status quo is our 'natural' state and for most of us, this is where we'll stay. I didn't want to stay there and from experience I knew that I was neither fulfilling nor building my potential.

Having studied human performance and more recently psychology, I am fascinated by what drives our thoughts, feelings and behaviours. This fascination led me to composing a collection of articles dealing with elements that influence our leadership, our performance and our overall well-being.

Leadership in terms of leading ourselves through personal development and leading others to assist them in building their potential.

Performance in terms of what motivates and encourages us to strive, to apply grit to our endeavours and to consistently achieve beyond the average.

Well-being in terms of psychological, physical and social resources that equip us to meet life's challenges.

What I have found is that building our potential is not difficult. In fact, when I reflected on the circumstances surrounding significant achievement and potential, I noticed a simple pattern.

Small, consistent actions done well, develop your potential.

What are these actions and what are the attributes that drive the way we think, feel and behave? This collection of articles offers valuable insight and will introduce you to practical, evidence-based concepts (grounded in neuroscience and psychology) that will have a positive impact on your leadership, your performance and your well-being. *And*, if applied whole-heartedly, you will most certainly build your potential.

PART I: LEADERSHIP

The traditional approach to leadership places human nature aside and focuses primarily on strategy and business results. Whilst these may be crucial and necessary capabilities, leaders must equip themselves with more appropriate tools for operating in todays' environment. Business in the 21st century has borrowed a term from the military, which it used to describe the world post-cold-war—VUCA—standing for an environment that is volatile, uncertain, complex and ambiguous. Add to this the consistency of change, along with the pace at which we are operating and leading top-down is not sustainable. Leaders today require the know-how to retain clarity and focus, to make the difficult decisions, to support their teams and cultivate a culture respective of autonomy, mastery and purpose. A culture that celebrates the individual contributor, high-performing teams and ongoing, continuous improvement.

Self-Actualisation = Leadership

When psychologist Carl Jung described the qualities self-actualised people possess, he wasn't linking these traits to leadership. He did however retrospectively highlight the likes of Martin Luther King, Helen Keller and Gandhi as prominent figures who personified the characteristics detailed below.

Self Actualised People Are:

1. Creative.
2. Spontaneous.
3. Accepting of themselves & others.
4. Self-Confident but not self-centered.
5. Based in reality and place their focus there.
6. Altruistic.
7. Satisfied with a few deep connections (have outgrown the need to be popular).
8. Not afraid to rock the boat.
9. Prone to peak experiences (seek risk).
10. In pursuit of knowledge.

Self-actualised people moreover, spend a significant amount of time in self-reflection; enabling ongoing, continuous improvement personally. This is aligned with Carol Dweck's concept of a growth mindset, which encourages individuals to regularly seek feedback and learn from their experiences. Dweck believes that the pursuit of knowledge is manifest in a hunger for learning; those with a growth mindset define success as getting smarter, as opposed to those with a fixed mindset who have the innate need to be right, all of the time. [1]

For the sake of this article, we'll explore one of the qualities we can instantly begin to nurture – self-confidence.

Self-confidence despite its lack of theoretical support, is a component of self-efficacy, which is defined by Albert Bandura as "an individual's belief (or confidence) about his or her abilities to mobilise motivation, cognitive resources, and courses of action needed to successfully execute a specific task within a given context". [2] Simply put, self-efficacy is the belief one has in one's abilities to thrive in a given situation.

According to Bandura, self-efficacy can be developed through mastery experiences, social modeling, verbal persuasion and psychological/physiological responses.

Translate these determinants into real-world applications and **individuals & leaders can dominate** if they:

- Seek opportunities for performance attainment (through setting goals beyond skill-set)
- Engage a mentor (with accomplishments who emulates self-efficacy)
- Find a fan (someone who supports you, praises your efforts and truly believes in you)
- Reframe stress. (get curious about the feeling and use it to your advantage) [3]

Leaders can also embrace these concepts within the organisation and foster the strength of self-efficacy, which has been linked to improvements in performance, motivation and overall well-being. [4] Self-efficacy also sits within the Positive Organisational Behavior model put forth by Luthans which further incorporates resilience, hope and optimism.

References

[1] Dweck, Carol S.. (2008) *Mindset :the new psychology of success* New York : Ballantine Books,
[2] Bandura, A. (1997). *Self-efficacy: The exercise of control*. New York: Freeman.
[3] McGonigal, K. *How to make stress your friend. TED talk.* https://www.ted.com/talks/kelly_mcgonigal_how_to_make_stress_your_friend
[4] Luthans, F., & Youssef, C. M. (2007). Emerging positive organizational behavior. *Journal of management, 33*(3), 321-349.

Well-being in Leadership

"You can't solve todays problems with yesterdays solutions."

Barbara Fredrickson

The notion of positive psychology in business is a concept that has garnered mixed reception. If all leaders understood that at its core, positive psychology focuses on strengths and establishes resources within human capital so that resilience, performance and overall well-being are maximised, more of them would definitely subscribe to the paradigms within.

To define well-being in leadership and substantiate how it can increase an individuals' leadership effectiveness, I refer to the construct of well-being provided by Martin Seligman ~ a thought-leader in the field. According to Seligmans' theory, well-being is comprised of 5 elements, each independent of themselves and pursued for their own right.

Elements of Well-being Model PERMA (Martin Seligman)

1. Positive Emotion
2. Engagement
3. Relationships
4. Meaning
5. Achievement

Positive Emotion

Making a conscious effort to focus on positive emotions provides individuals with an optimistic view the past, present, and future. This in turn is linked to improvements in resilience, creativity, innovation, engagement and overall sense of satisfaction. [1]

Positive emotions are not merely the hedonic feelings of pleasure, but include feelings of joy, gratitude, serenity, hope, interest, pride, amusement, inspiration, awe and love. [2]

Leaders would benefit from understanding their own extent of positive emotions as well as ways they could evoke positive emotions within their teams and across their organisation.

Engagement

The work of Mihaly Csikzentmihalyi examines engagement through the state of flow ~ being totally immersed in an activity, one that challenges but is not too demanding or too simple. When individuals find themselves in this state, they become so absorbed in the activity it is timeless, creativity and effort are high, and they are playing to their strengths. Engagement can play to athletic, creative, cognitive or signature strengths.

If leaders played to their strengths and provided an environment for team members to utilise their strengths, performance and energy levels would simultaneously increase. If managers challenged their team members and set appropriate goals, the state of flow would be more attainable.

Relationships

'Other people matter' a statement by Christopher Peterson, epitomises the need for positive relationships. Having positive connections with other people has been linked to things such as improved ability to deal with stress, greater levels of collaboration, better physical and mental health.

Leaders would clearly benefit from having positive relationships themselves, and promoting positive connections and social capital across the organisation. Mentors are one way organisations have started doing this, team meetings also promote positive connections within smaller teams. There are many ways to elevate positive relationships within the workplace.

Meaning

Working towards something bigger than one's self is how meaning is described in the literature. Meaning can come from several sources such as achievement, relationships, altruism, spirituality and justice. [3] Meaning also incorporates living aligned with one's values.

Creative work, opportunity for achievement and personal growth are just a few avenues organisations can tap into in order to provide more meaning in the workplace. Leaders must also take this into perspective so that they continue to have meaning in their day-to-day operations, as all too often they are inclined to get caught up in the numbers and the bottom-line.

Achievement/Accomplishment

Having goals and working towards something energises, influences our motivational systems, and leads to higher levels of self-efficacy[4]. Simple rituals such as making your bed each morning, contribute to your sense of achievement. Carol Dweck determined that the power of our mindset directly impacts our goal setting and likelihood of attainment.[5]

Achievement in the workplace may appear an easy element to implement however, there are many things leaders can be doing to increase their teams/ organisations sense of achievement. Breaking down goals into smaller tasks provides small wins along the way, contributing to overall well-being. Setting rituals at team meetings and for basic processes also contributes to sense of achievement. Having weekly, monthly and quarterly expectations and discussions are other means of contributing to overall sense of achievement. Incorporating personal goals and wellness objectives addresses the work-life integration that should be considered in todays integrated world.

5 Things Leaders Can Do to Increase Overall Well-being

1. Raise awareness of their own levels of positive emotion, engagement, positive relationships, meaning and achievement.
2. Drive a strengths based culture.
3. Harness and encourage curiosity and creativity.
4. Provide opportunities for ongoing development.
5. Set challenging yet attainable goals.

To clarify, well-being is not wellness, however it definitely contributes to it. As a small insight into well-being in leadership, **PERMA** can be one of the constructs utilised for improving leadership impact **and** an organisations inclusive well-being.

References

[1] Biswas-Diener, R & Dean, B. (2007) Positive Psychology Coaching. Wiley & Sons, UK
[2] Fredrickson, Barbara L. "Positive emotions." *Handbook of positive psychology* (2002): 120-134.
[3] Wong, 1998, Fry, Prem S. (Ed), (1998). The human quest for meaning: A handbook of psychological research and clinical applications. , (pp. 111-140). Mahwah, NJ, US: Lawrence Erlbaum Associates Publishers, xxvi, 462 pp.
[4] Bandura 1997 Self Efficacy: The Exercise of Control. Worth Publishers.
[5] Dweck, C. 2008. Mindset: The New Psychology of Success. Random House Publishers.

Other

https://www.psychologytoday.com/articles/199707/finding-flow
https://www.health.harvard.edu/newsletter_article/the-health-benefits-of-strong-relationships
http://www.positivepsyc.com/blog/the-meaning-of-life-the-m-in-perma

What Golf Can Teach Us About Mindset & Leadership

Even the worlds' best golfers have the occasional bad hit.

A seemingly secure advantage is surrendered and inexplicably the game plan begins to unravel. Talent, flair and discipline suddenly take a back seat and the champion becomes human again, misjudging the distance and landing in the bunker.

The question is "what happens next ?"

It is at this defining moment that the true athlete buckles down and proceeds to grind out the win. However, this isn't always the case. Occasionally we are witness to a meltdown, as the result of a break in concentration, a temporary loss of finesse.

What delineates these two potential outcomes? **Mindset**.

According to Carol Dweck, the Stanford psychologist who has spent several decades studying human behaviour ~specifically in relation to success and achievement ~ there are two distinct mindsets individuals may possess. A fixed mindset, in which the individual believes their basic qualities are fixed traits and a growth mindset, in which the individual believes their basic qualities can be developed through dedication and hard work. This isn't to say the golfer who had the meltdown hasn't worked hard to get where he/she is. However, once faced with adversity or failure, the break in concentration is likely due to a thought that has crept in, creating doubt in their own ability and/or their likelihood of winning. This thought could be anything from 'I never hit well out of the sand' to 'I always break under pressure', or potentially be a deep seated fear of failure. This thought is the product of a fixed mindset.

A growth mindset, on the other hand, embraces both challenge and adversity, recognising them as opportunities for improvement. The thought pattern of an individual with a growth mindset in the same situation may look like this: 'Bugger, oh well, I can learn from this shot and apply what I know from previous experience' or 'this is where I come into my own, I thrive on these difficult hits'. Failure is not feared by those with a growth mindset, but merely as further opportunity to improve.

In golf, as in life, mindset fluctuates and varies from one activity to the next. The good news is that we have the ability to nurture and develop a growth mindset within ourselves and in others, the million-dollar question is how?

How to Develop a Growth Mindset

1. Develop an awareness. Research has demonstrated that having an awareness and general understanding about the brain and its plasticity is the starting point for changing from a fixed mindset to a growth mindset. [1] We now know that the brain is like a muscle, when we use it, it gets stronger. The more effort we put into things, the stronger the connections between our brain cells/neurons become. Tiger Woods has experienced an overhaul on his swing 4 times in his career. He had to re-learn the mechanics (building new neural pathways) and step outside his comfort zone in order to progress; all in the pursuit of growth and continuous improvement.

As leaders, we should encourage employees to try new things, challenge themselves and operate outside of their comfort zones. As organisations we should hire for potential and be confident that we can cultivate talent.

2. Be curious. When things go awry, rather than getting frustrated and holding onto the inner critic, we should ask ourselves why things went wrong and seek feedback. Developing ritual questions we ask ourselves in the face of failure is a good way to harness this curiosity. This is the very reason golfers analyse their swing through video over and over again and the reason they change coaches so often. They are in search of what aspect of their swing is going wrong when they mishit the ball and seek feedback on how to adjust accordingly. When things go wrong, leadership expert Jim Collins found that leaders of successful organisations demonstrated curiosity and interest, attempting to understand what took place during the process and offer further support. [2]

As leaders, rather than focusing purely on success within the organisation, evidence suggests failure tolerant leaders routinely focus on increasing intellectual capital.

3. Be accountable. There are golfers on the tour who attribute blame to everything and everyone but themselves when things are less than perfect. Psychologists have even coined the phrase 'frustrated golfers syndrome'. Phil Mickelson is the classic example of this where blame is directed insidiously at course designers, other players and other variables as far fetched as 'curses'. Your motivation and your ability lie within your domain, you are responsible for both. Accepting this and taking responsibility for the process of continuous improvement is critical to developing a growth mindset. Sports writer Bill Rand says that Tiger Woods speaks constantly about his commitment to the process of his swing and candidly talks about his short comings.

As leaders, providing team members with autonomy, mastery and purpose (as Daniel Pink suggests) creates an environment of accountability. [3]

4. Have a plan & put the effort in. In order to sustain any type of change/improvement, you need a plan. This is where rituals become essential and deliberate practice of the desired behaviour is inherent, ongoing and constantly refined. When golfers review the course layout, they make a plan and they practice the plan. They visualise the course, visualise their swing, their contact with the ball, their flawless execution. They then practice for each possible scenario of what might go wrong.

In an ideal world, leaders would not only present the strategy, but also put the honest effort in to get everyone on board. The plan needs to be constantly tweaked to adjust for shifting market dynamics. So often leaders get caught up in the end goal, thereby neglecting the journey, forgetting about the people and what really matters.

Change isn't easy, the good news is that it's possible. Understanding that whilst it's possible to develop a growth mindset, it will present challenges. It requires effort and the intangible quality psychologist Angela Duckworth calls GRIT. Be curious, be accountable and your passion and perseverance will pay dividends, in life and in golf.

References

[1] Dweck, Carol. Mindset: Changing the way you think to fulfil your potential. Little Brown Book Group, 2012.
[2] Collins, Jim. Good to Great. Harpers Collins Publishers, 2005.
[3] Pink, Daniel. Drive: The surprising truth about what motivates us. Canongate Books, 2011.

Other

https://hbr.org/2002/08/the-failure-tolerant-leader
https://www.psychologytoday.com/blog/what-is-he-thinking/200904/frustrated-golfer-syndrome-causes-and-cures
https://www.ted.com/talks/angela_lee_duckworth_grit_the_power_of_passion_and_perseverance?language=en

Leadership Through Challenge & Change

We've all been there, the organisation/manager you are working for is under pressure to perform or a significant restructure is in the cards and our autonomy and/or career are under threat. The number one action leaders should be taking is communicating however, this is where they are often failing. Non-existent or poor communication is rampant across organisations, leading to a decline in engagement, performance and most significantly trust in leadership.

George a long-time employee and marketing manager of a large global corporate was told that he would be moving with the sale of his business, to the company that bought it. That was the communication. After fifteen years of service he was told what was going to happen, not consulted, not comforted, not considered. His direct line manager avoided eye contact with him in the office for the next few weeks, the managing director said nothing as he passed him in the corridor. Really? Is this how loyal, hard-working, long-time employees should be treated? Or was there a better way of going about this?

Rachel – a senior manager is under pressure from the new GM to achieve an unrealistic sales target; she starts micromanaging her tenured team. Her expectations become irrational and inconsiderate, she appears stressed and tired all of the time. The team begin consoling one another and then they begin to leave or worse yet switch-off. Could Rachel have approached this differently?

In both of these real-world scenarios, the communication was poor and there's a good chance through further scrutiny that the ratio of positive-to-negative verbal and non-verbal behaviour was low. Social psychologists have been studying positive and negative interactions in the workplace and marriages and can with incredible accuracy (in a very short amount of time) can predict workplace performance and divorce. The positive-to-negative ratio (PNR) is the method they utilise to develop their predictions and it's essentially the amount of positive interactions compared to negative.

Studies have shown that in marriages the magic number is 5:1 and in the workplace high performing teams have a ratio of 5.6:1.

So looking back on George's experience what approach would have offered the best outcome? Open and honest discussions with George (and his team) leading up to the sale of the business would have been a good start. Including the team in these conversations would have given them a sense of inclusion and that would have contributed to increased engagement and feelings of inclusion. When there is silence surrounding an issue or a change it leaves people feeling insignificant, helpless and under-valued. Approaching change from a positive perspective could have been executed through a high PNR as well as the 4-D model of appreciative inquiry which offers a platform of appreciation, empowerment, inspiration, and positive change.

Rachel's manager could have sat down with the team, discussed the challenges and collaborated to reach a positive approach. Her manager needed the skills of self-awareness and self-compassion prior to communicating negatively with her team.

Negativity restricts and breeds mistrust whereas positivity (according to Barbara Fredrickson and colleagues) leads to expansion and broadening of thought-action repertoires.

With this knowledge of positive-negative ratios, leaders should start paying closer attention to their communication and the interactions they have [as well as across their organisations]. Increasing positive emotions and communications can lead to many things, above all significant increases in well-being, performance and trust in leadership. Definitely something to consider when change and uncertainty are prolific.

References

https://www.gottman.com/blog/the-workplace-the-ideal-praise-to-criticism-ratio/
http://www.davidcooperrider.com/ai-process/

Neuroleadership: Increase Your Impact

An elusive construct, neuroleadership has caught the attention of the corporate world, from senior executives looking for ways to strengthen their leadership impact, to individual contributors looking to sharpen the saw on their performance. Regardless of position or profile, neuroleadership is an approach to leadership that can offer benefits to the masses.

There are a host of neuroleadership theories, however, collectively the underlying principal is two-fold: understand how leaders can reach optimal performance through harnessing the empirical evidence in neuroscience AND subsequently identify how these leaders can cultivate optimal performance in those that they lead (formally or informally) through this evidence.

So what does the science say? Our brain, as complex as it is, is also quite simple when it comes to performance. Give it the right fuel, provide it with ample rest, and exercise it through cognitive and physical activities, and it will deliver its best. Scientists have also identified neural pathways and neurotransmitters (hormones) that foster our ability to focus, determine sources for motivation and reward, and drive curiosity/innovation. Some of these same pathways are also responsible for our executive functioning, self-regulation and emotion regulation ~ all essential skills when it comes to leadership and overall performance at work.

Let's break this down:

FUEL: The latest evidence confirms that what we eat has a direct influence on our cognition and our emotions. Certain types of food also increase our ability to concentrate, problem solve and store memories whereas others IE transfats* and sugars ~ have demonstrated their potential to impair these abilities. A mediterranean diet (rich in whole grains, fruit, leafy greens, beans, nuts olive oil, small portions of chicken and fish) has been linked to positive brain function, higher energy levels and correspondingly decreases in cognitive decline and cellular ageing. Hydration is also a key component when it comes to the brains performance: a mere 1% dehydration has been correlated with adverse effects on cognitive performance.

REST: John Lehrer writes in his book – Imagine: How Creativity Works – that without brain-breaks, we inhibit the sort of creative connections that lead to breakthroughs. It is also known that the area in our brain primarily responsible for decision making, focus and self-regulation (the prefrontal cortex) has limited energy; it requires rest in order to perform. According to Ferris Jabr in his systematic review, "downtime replenishes the brain's stores of attention and motivation, encourages productivity and creativity, and is essential to both achieve our highest levels of performance and simply form stable memories in everyday life". Furthermore, when our brains are at rest, our memories are being consolidated and our neural pathways are being reinforced.

Top Hacks for Resting Your Brain

1. Take a nap (a 7–10 minute nap can increase alertness for up to 3 hours)
2. Meditate (decreases activity in prefrontal cortex which increases focus, EQ and executive functioning)
3. Let your mind wander. (increases your ability to solve problems)

EXERCISE: Increasing blood-flow to the brain through exercise not only provides the brain with more oxygen, but it also releases a variety of hormones related to our motivation and reward systems. The best type of exercise is typically any form that gets your heart pumping (aerobic), however, certain dance styles have been shown to provide additional benefit due to both the physical and mental demands. Aside from oxygen and hormone activation, aerobic exercise also creates BDNF (brain derived neurotropic factor) which according to Dr. John Ratey, keeps our brain cells young and prepares our brains for neuroplasticity.

NEURAL PATHWAYS & NEUROTRANSMITTERS: A neural pathway is a network of brain cells that communicate through neurotransmitters (hormones that initiate communication within brain cells). Scientists have discovered a reward and reinforcement system/pathway which leads to motivation through the release of dopamine (feel-good neurotransmitter). Dopamine reinforces the behaviour through the pleasure feeling it provides and also activates memory so that the behaviour can be repeated, as long as it takes the right pathway. At work, the brain can be rewarded with dopamine through things such as incremental goals and positive feedback. Founder of the Neuroleadership Institute David Rock has developed the SCARF model which emphasises the brains inclination towards reward and away from threat, creating self and social awareness. Within an organisation leaders should seek to provide individuals with autonomy, choice, certainty, relatedness and have a corporate sense of fairness – all of which contribute to engagement, motivation and discretionary efforts.

In closing, developing a simple awareness about the brain, nourishing the brain as suggested above with the right fuel, rest & exercise, and creating space for reflection and attention training (IE mindfulness), enables leaders to make better decisions, stay calm under pressure, and maximise their leadership impact.

*Transfats are unsaturated fats that act like saturated fats and can be found in high levels in foods such as pastries, frozen pizza, commercial cakes and biscuits, deep fried foods.

References

Lehrer, Jonathan. (2012). Imagine: How creativity works. Houghton Mifflin Harcourt, Boston.
https://www.ncbi.nlm.nih.gov/pmc/articles/PMC2805706/
https://www.ncbi.nlm.nih.gov/pmc/articles/PMC3280054/
http://www.health.com/mind-body/mediterranean-diet-improves-memory
https://www.ncbi.nlm.nih.gov/pubmed/17921465
https://www.scientificamerican.com/article/mental-downtime/
https://www.ncbi.nlm.nih.gov/pubmed/21075238
https://www.forbes.com/sites/alicegwalton/2015/02/09/7-ways-meditation-can-actually-change-the-brain/#4cb284171465

https://www.psychologytoday.com/blog/the-power-daydreaming/201004/
    mind-wandering-enhances-creative-problem-solving
https://www.youtube.com/watch?v=hBSVZdTQmDs
https://www.quora.com/What-is-the-neural-basis-of-motivation
https://www.epa.gov/sites/production/files/2015-09/documents/thurs_
    georgia_9_10_915_covello.pdf

Mindful Leadership: Your 'Connection'

Clarity, focus, creativity, and compassion: these are the fundamentals of mindful leadership according to Janice Marturano, founder and executive director of the not for profit Institute for Mindful Leadership and author of Finding the Space to Lead. Janice whilst a VP and deputy general counsel at General Mills, found herself burning the candle at both ends and eventually reached a point in her career/life where she no longer felt 'connected' to what mattered. Following an executive mindfulness retreat, Janice experienced a significant shift in her leadership capabilities (and her life) and was so impacted by the program that she initiated a mindful leadership program within the company.

Michael Bunting, founder of The Mindful Leader and author of the same book has spent over 16 years teaching mindful leadership to business and government. Michael suggests 7 disciplines of mindful leaders which are summarised as: presence, accountability, mindful values, mindful vision, curiosity/innovation mindset, empowering others and nourishing others. Michael believes that your effectiveness as a leader can be strengthened through mindfulness offering 'positive and meaningful impact'.

A regular mindfulness practice has been linked to improvements in each of the fundamentals and disciplines mentioned above and *more*. Yet in some circles its' contribution remains criticised. Studies have demonstrated significant changes in brain structure, behaviour and emotional intelligence and those who adopt a regular practice and persevere through any of the doubt, soon realise the innate potential mindfulness offers. As a leader how can you harness the potential of mindfulness so that it bolsters your leadership impact?

Leadership is no longer solely about leading others, it's about leading yourself and managing the complexities and uncertainties of the workplace (and life) during a time when organisations are rife with change. Leaders need solutions for todays problems and they need support beyond 'strategic imperatives' and 'leadership competencies'. Above all else, leaders need to be and feel *connected* to their teams, their customers and most importantly themselves.

"Human connection is the key to personal & professional success."
Paul J. Meyer

Having worked with multiple leaders across a number of organisations and industries this past year, and from my own personal journey, I have found that the most significant impact of mindfulness lies within this "*connection*" to self and others. It's easy and more common than not to get caught up in the busyness of work and life, resorting to autopilot to get things done. Unfortunately, what this can lead to is an erosion of empathy and *connection* to the self and others.

Perspective What mindfulness offers is an opportunity to press the pause button in order to gain some perspective (Langer, 1992). As a leader you need to offer an unbiased perspective, avoiding mindsets that limit, and if you're *connected* to your thoughts, behaviours and feelings there's a better chance of ensuring this as a reality.

Decision Making As a leader, the number of decisions you make in a single day prove to be not only exhausting but borderline overwhelming. Unless you're *connected* to yourself and *connected* to others, all of these decisions only become cumbersome and feared, resulting in poor choices and potentially burnout.

Emotional Intelligence As a leader you need to rely on others for their guidance, support and following, and if you neglect to have that *connection* to self and others, your emotional intelligence (EI) in terms of self-awareness, self-regulation and insight suffers. Mindfulness has been demonstrated to raise EI and improve relationships (Siegel, 2007).

Stress Management The reality is 85% of Australian workers will experience work-related stress over the next 12months resulting in 20 million sick days. Termed the 'silent killer' stress can lead to a number of chronic conditions and can likewise become detrimental to your leadership capability.

Learning to manage perceptions of stress and equipping yourself with the resources to adequately recover from stress is mandatory. Being *connected* to your 'self' allows you to recognise the physiological and psychological manifestations of stress as soon as they appear and respond in a way that supports your perception and your recovery. Mindfulness has been linked to lasting decrease in psychological symptoms related to stress, anxiety and depression.

Empathy A newcomer to the list of leadership must-haves, empathy is what separates the great from the good. In a project run at Google to determine what produced the most effective teams, empathy was singled out as a necessary capacity which afforded psychological safety, improved collaboration and enhanced problem solving. From healthcare workers to CEO's, practicing mindfulness can increase levels of empathy and compassion. Mindfulness creates a platform for *connecting* to ones self and to others in an authentic, unbiased, supportive manner.

What Now?

So where do you begin? You're time-poor as it is and adding yet another 'productivity hack' to your list of things to do seems daunting. The good news is you can add mindfulness to your day without it taking up any additional time! Start with a mindful breath ~ you're already breathing, just pay attention to the air as it enters and leaves, breathing in and out of your nostrils. 6 seconds is all it takes to initiate the 'relaxation response' which releases the neurotransmitter acetylcholine into your system calming everything down, reducing reactivity, slowing your heart rate and lowering your blood pressure (it also assists in memory and learning). Apply mindfulness to everyday activities such as showering, brushing your teeth, eating or walking. If you want to take the next step, there are a number of APPs and resources available to begin a regular mindfulness practice which can be found here. (https://www.cortexconsulting.com.au/books).

The thing about mindfulness is like anything that you what to improve, it needs to be practiced, and practiced deliberately and regularly. Mindful leadership does offer the individual and organisation a myriad of benefits through *connection* and if done right, it has the ability to sharpen your mind and strengthen your business.

> "Mindfulness is awareness that arises through paying attention,
> on purpose, in the present moment, non-judgementally."
>
> *Jon Kabat-Zinn*

References

Brown, K. W., & Ryan, R. M. (2003). The benefits of being present: mindfulness and its role in psychological well-being. *Journal of personality and social psychology, 84*(4), 822.

Davidson RJ, Kabat-Zinn J, Schumacher J, et al. (2003).Alterations in brain and immune function produced by mindfulness meditation, Psychosomatic Medicine , 65 (pg. 564-70)

Gratz, K. L., & Tull, M. T. (2010). Emotion regulation as a mechanism of change in acceptance-and mindfulness-based treatments. *Assessing mindfulness and acceptance processes in clients: Illuminating the theory and practice of change*, 107-133.

Langer, E. J. (1992). Matters of mind: Mindfulness/mindlessness in perspective. *Consciousness and cognition, 1*(3), 289-305.

Lazrus, Sarah et al. (2005). Meditation experience is associated with increased cortical thickness. *Neuroreport.* 16(17): 1893–1897.

Siegel, D. (2007). Mindfulness training and neural integration: differentiation of distinct streams of awareness and the cultivation of well-being. *Social Cognitive Affective Neuroscience*, 2 (4): 259-263.

https://www.mindfulleaderbook.com/

https://www.ncbi.nlm.nih.gov/pmc/articles/PMC2527776/

https://academic.oup.com/scan/article/2/4/259/1676806

http://www.medibank.com.au/about-us/media-centre-details. aspx?news=520

http://www.sciencedirect.com/science/article/pii/S0022399903005737

https://www.nytimes.com/2016/02/28/magazine/what-google-learned-from-its-quest-to-build-the-perfect-team.html?_r=0

5 Steps to Positively Engage Your Organisation

There seems to be a great deal of discussion centered around employee engagement of late, likely stimulated by the publication of the Gallup report indicating that a mere 13% of employees are 'engaged' globally. Whilst organisations attempt to address this issue through surveys and project teams, there are many other courses of action that could be undertaken, with strong evidence supporting the high impact outcomes they propose.

Workplace engagement has been defined as: "when employees feel positive emotions toward their work, find their work to be personally meaningful, consider their workload to be manageable, and have hope about the future of their work" [1]. This is directly proportional to the fact that the needs of the workforce are changing, with employees seeking more meaningful work and the opportunity for ongoing personal and skill development. Organisations can easily tap into these needs and explore the options for meeting them.

The mindful implementation of the following offers those enlightened organisations a wealth of opportunity to build cultural strength and develop individual capacity.

5 Steps of Positive Engagement

1. Create an environment that fosters **positive emotions** such as curiosity, pride, gratitude, love, contentment and joy. According to leading psychologist Barbara Fredrickson, certain positive emotions broaden people's thought-action repertoires, leading to enduring personal resources.[2] This has consequently led to enhanced resilience, relationships, well-being and satisfaction.

2. Acknowledge and harness individual employee **strengths**. The Corporate Leadership Council determined through an analysis of >19,000 employees, that when managers focused on performance strengths, there was a 36.4% increase in performance. [3] Addi-

tional benefits of utilising strengths include increases in well-being, confidence, energy, resilience, engagement, happiness and goal attainment. [4] Donald Clifton from Gallup has also determined that individuals who use their strengths daily feel 6x more engaged than those who don't.

3. Ensure **appropriate development plans** are in place and reviewed regularly. So often plans are made at the beginning of the year, a box is ticked and said plans are not referred to until the end of the year, with little or no follow-up in between. Employees enjoy stimulation, particularly challenges that sit outside of their comfort zone and daily operations which nurture their development. Managers need to proactively initiate development conversations and cultivate an environment for ongoing, continuous learning within their team.

4. Provide **meaningful goals.** Goals that are aligned with the strategic vision as well as the individuals strengths, are more likely to produce positive outcomes. Utilise the SMART framework however definitely get creative and be as specific as you can with the actions you are going to take in order to achieve your goals. Use verbs and identify feelings you desire upon achieving your goal.(IE: Invite 5 new connections each week on social media to broaden my network and build the foundation for my business success=happiness/pride). (see book *Desire Map* on creating goals with soul)

5. Implement a **well-being program** to encourage and promote mental health. With workplace anxiety on the rise and 85% of Australian workers facing stress, organisations must address this ever-growing concern. Whilst well-being incorporates positive emotions, it also focuses on engagement, positive relationships, meaning and achievement. The opportunities for developing well-being at work are numerous and should be explored further.

The steps above offer simple, effective solutions to engagement concerns in addition to providing a host of other benefits to individuals and organisations.

References

[1] Macey, W. & Schneider, B. (2008). The meaning of employee engagement. Industrial and Organizational Psychology: Perspectives on Science and Practice, 1(1), 3-30.

[2] Fredrickson, B. The role of positive emotions in positive psychology: The broaden-and-build theory of positive emotions. American Psychologist, Vol 56(3), Mar 2001, 218-226

[3] Corporate Leadership Council 2003. Building the High-Performance Workforce A Quantitative Analysis of the Effectiveness of Performance Management Strategies. Washington, DC.

[4] Govindji, R., & Linley, P. A. (2007). Strengths use, self-concordance and well-being: Implications for strengths coaching and coaching psychologists. International Coaching Psychology Review, 2 (2), 143-153.;

[5] Linley, P. A., Nielsen, K. M., Wood, A. M., Gillett, R., & Biswas-Diener, R., (2010). Using signature strengths in pursuit of goals: Effects on goal progress, need satisfaction, and well-being, and implications for coaching psychologists. International Coaching Psychology Review, 5 (1), 8-17.

PART 2: PERFORMANCE

I'm always looking for ways to improve my performance both physically and mentally, I know that I have more in the tank to give and I am striving to reach my potential. Healthy striving, not obsessive, all-or-nothing striving. From biohacking to adjusting our cognitive appraisal, to improving our critical thinking ~ we are consistently striving for better, faster, stronger. Time has become a commodity for us all and looking for efficiencies and better ways of doing things has become inherent in our nature. Challenge yourself every day to perform better than you did the day before and you will create a winning mindset and achieve more. Just don't forget to enjoy the journey and the moments of just being, you need to fill the tank every now and then.

Everyday Success = GRIT + Self-Control

Tenacity, persistence, endurance, dogged determination. Qualities to seek out when recruiting high talent, merits to employ when pursuing goals, assets to harness when chasing your dreams.

Elite athletes possess these traits, as do high performing business people or essentially anyone excelling in their chosen domain. Everyday success also fosters these qualities, but what are they really? Moreover, how do you develop them?

Through her research in achievement and success, Angela Duckworth, (professor of psychology at the University of Pennsylvania) found there were two obvious determinants of success: *self-control and grit.*

According to Duckworth, self-control is the capacity to regulate attention, emotion and behaviour in the presence of temptation. [1] Self-control is called upon when there are two conflicting action tendencies (such as impulses) and the prefrontal brain areas become involved in top-down regulation; one of these impulses is affiliated with short-term gain and gratification whilst the other is geared toward enduring values and long-term goals. [2]

Grit has been defined as 'perseverance and passion for long-term goals' [3] and further research has indicated that grit predicts the achievement of these goals despite obstacles and setbacks. Evidence suggests that self-control is related more to every-day success whereas grit is affiliated with long-term goal attainment. However, both contribute to overall success due to the nature of goal orientation and attainment.

Fortunately psychologists and scientists alike have discovered that both self-control and grit can be developed, meaning it's never to late to pursue your goals and achieve your dreams. Let's explore how!

Ways to Cultivate Self-Control

1. **Regularly employ your willpower**. Having the ability to delay gratification is willpower at its essence. Like a muscle, your willpower gets stronger the more that you use it. Further, researchers have discovered that the more individuals employed willpower as children, the more self-control they possessed as adults, leading to greater success in life. [4] What's more, is the prefrontal cortex area of the brain appeared more active in individuals when they were employing willpower VS those who were not. This is the area responsible for self-regulation, emotion regulation, executive functioning & empathy.

2. **Be mindful**. Neuroscientists have demonstrated that a regular meditation practice leads to changes in our brain structure. One of these changes is an increase in grey matter in the prefrontal cortex, along with the anterior cingulate cortex (responsible for decision making and emotion regulation) and the hippocampus (responsible for learning and memory). Strengthening these ares through meditation has been directly correlated with improvements in self-regulation, EQ, memory and motivation. [5]

3. **Set milestones** of smaller goals that spiral up into larger goals. Having incremental achievements along the path to the end goal releases dopamine in the brain and provides a sense of pride. Dopamine has several affects on self-control, one of which is it's influence on the anterior cingulate cortex in relation to cognitive flexibility and control. [6] Pride is a positive emotion that is associated with our accomplishments and an increase in confidence to expand our belief in our potential to do greater things. This in turn broadens our perspective of what we can achieve and as a result, we achieve more.

Ways to Develop GRIT

1. **Foster a growth mindset.** Carol Dwecks' research on mindset identifies a growth mindset as that which believes growth is possible through learning, that which embraces challenge, believes effort is essential and that which views failure/setbacks as opportunity. Duckworth believes that a growth mindset is imperative if endeavouring to nurture grit, and it's understandable why.

2. **Keep the end in mind.** So often we get caught up in the complexities of our day, that our attention gets derailed and we neglect to focus on our end goal. Keeping our vision front of mind has been linked to goal attainment and success and writing our goals down is the key. Aside from writing our goals down, sharing our goals with others also increases our likelihood of attaining them. Gail Matthews found that individuals who shared weekly updates with colleagues/friends were more than 70 percent likely to accomplish their goal (completely accomplished their goal or were more than half way there), compared to 35 percent of those who kept their goals to themselves, without writing them down.

3. **Do what you love.** The very definition of grit includes the word passion. This suggests that if you are truly interested in what you are doing and continue to cultivate that interest, you are more likely to achieve success. Find something that inspires you and use that inspiration (another positive emotion) to broaden your perspective and stay true to your path. Barbara Fredricksons' broaden & build theory confirms that positive emotions open us up and provide us with enduring psychological, intellectual, physical and social resources. [7]

In closing, we are in the fortunate position of knowing that employing self-control and grit can lead us to success **and** we know that each of these behaviours can be developed. However, the ambiguity of human nature remains our challenge. Dr. Libby recently supported this notion at the Mindful Leadership Forum when she said "why is it we do what we do when we know what we know?".

Start playing on your own team and the odds will be in your favour. Channel those positive emotions and strengthen your probability of success.

References

[1] Duckworth, A. & Gross, J. Self Control and Grit: Related but separable determinants of success. Current Directions in Psychological Science October 2014 vol. 23 no. 5319-325

[2] Maglio, S. J., Trope, Y., & Liberman, N. (2013). The common currency of psychological distance. Current Directions in Psychological Science, 22, 278–282

[3] Duckworth, A., Peterson, C., Matthews, M & Kelly, C. GRIT: Perseverance and passion for long-term goals. Journal of Personality and Social Psychology, 2007, Vol. 92, No. 6, 1087–1101.

[4] Casey, B. J., et al. (2011). Behavioral and neural correlates of delay of gratification 40 years later. Proceedings of the National Academy of Sciences, 108(36), 14998–15003

[5] Lykins, E. & Baer, R. (2009) Psychological funcitioning in a sample of long-term practitioners of mindfulness meditation. Journal of Cognitive Psychotherapy: An International Quarterly Volume 23, Number 3 ; Langer, E. J. (1997). The power of mindful learning. Reading, MA: Addison Wesley.

[6] Ashby, F. Gregory; Isen, Alice M.; Turken, A neuropsychological theory of positive affect and its influence on cognition. Psychological Review, Vol 106(3), Jul 1999, 529-550.

[7] Fredrickson, Barbara (2001). The role of positive emotions in positive psychology: The broaden-and-build theory of positive emotions. .American Psychologist, Vol 56(3), Mar 2001, 218-226

Staying Focused & Energised

269 billion emails are sent and received each day across the globe! On some days, if you're anything like me, it feels like a significant proportion of those emails are headed directly to *your* inbox. As if this wasn't enough, we now grapple with the management of our social media, these platforms monopolising on average 1-2 hours of each working day. We face incessant interruption in the workplace (every 3 minutes) and working on "projects" that sit outside of our "role" has become the new norm. Combine this with your life outside of work and you have little, if any, down time. Our energy levels appear to be at an all-time low and our focus is fleeting. Despite getting a full-nights sleep we wake-up exhausted....why?

The pace and amount of information we contend with on a daily basis are the culprits for the exhaustion we are feeling as a society. When your energy levels are down and you find yourself constantly task-switching or off with the fairies ~ *your* work, *your*relationships and *your* health collectively suffer.

The latest trends in the health and well-being space all seem to incorporate self-care, better sleep and improved recovery and that's no coincidence. The good news is there are a few minor adjustments you can make to increase your focus and raise your energy throughout the day.

One of the areas in our brain responsible for focusing is the prefrontal cortex (PFC) ~ also known as the 'executive centre' of our brain. Just like your car, the prefrontal cortex runs out of fuel (approximately every 2 hours) whilst at the same time using a large proportion of the energy/food we consume (similar to the engine of a petrol guzzling sports car). Aside from focusing, the PFC is also responsible for decision making, problem solving, planning, multi-tasking, emotion regulation, discipline, and working memory. When the PFC is exhausted, all of these capacities are negatively affected as well.

The habits suggested below all support your PFC so that it functions optimally whilst ensuring your energy levels and focus remain high.

Habits To Stay Focused & Lift Your Energy

1. **Add 'buffers' into your day** ~ schedule time in your calendar for yourself throughout your day to think, reflect and connect with others. This time will become invaluable and will even reduce multi-tasking which has been shown to decrease our brains efficiency by as much as 40%.

2. **Hydrate** ~ as little as 1% dehydration effects the performance of your brain. Drinking 2-3L of water a day has countless benefits including enhancements in physical performance, energy and brain function.

3. **Fuel** ~ regular snacking on brain friendly foods will ensure your energy levels are stable. Seeds and nuts, protein, fruit and folate rich greens all stimulate the release of dopamine which contributes to alertness, creativity and concentration,

4. **Exercise** ~ this appears in almost every post I write, I'm a huge advocate for physical training (my P.E background kicking in!). Getting your heart rate up sends blood to your brain which does two things: it provides fresh, oxygenated blood to your brain AND it stimulates neurogenesis (creation of new brain cells). Win-win!

5. **Rest** ~ Every 90 minutes take a break from whatever it is that you're doing. Walk around, stretch, replenish, get some fresh air and breathe. Beyond a 'break' rest includes day-dreaming, certain types of meditation (IE yoga nidra) and sleep. Your body and brain both need to recover and making time for these activities is paramount to your performance. Sleep pods? Yes please – napping increases mental operations, performance and reaction times and 10-15 minutes is all you need.

"The buffer is the best investment you can make in yourself and the single most important productivity tool I use."

Jeff Weiner

It will be much easier to introduce these habits into your day *if* you focus on the outcome, your *why* behind them. Yes, you want to increase your ability to focus and raise your energy levels, but *why* do you want to do that? Continue asking yourself and you'll eventually get to the underlying values that will ultimately drive your behaviour.

References

http://www.radicati.com/wp/wp-content/uploads/2017/01/Email-Statistics-Report-2017-2021-Executive-Summary.pdf

https://www.fastcompany.com/1701850/how-social-media-has-changed-workplace-study

https://www.fastcompany.com/944128/worker-interrupted-cost-task-switching

http://www.authenticityassociates.com/brain-power-the-cause-of-focus/

https://medium.com/bsxtechnologies/4-ways-dehydration-affects-your-brain-e4042a6cb6b1

https://www.mindbodygreen.com/0-4287/10-Reasons-Why-You-Should-Drink-More-Water.html

https://bebrainfit.com/increase-dopamine/

http://www.abc.net.au/health/library/stories/2009/07/23/2633472.htm

http://www.executivestyle.com.au/why-you-need-a-nana-nap-2pf4n

Deliberate Practice Makes Perfect

Upon the arrival of our baby boy, I shared with my husband a few of the hopes that I had for him: to play soccer, tennis and golf ~ the "money" sports I termed them. They also happened to be the sports that would protect him from the ravages of rugby, ice hockey and AFL (cue boos from fellow Canadians and Aussies). I started reading about the parenting styles and behaviours required to cultivate an environment for the next Cristiano Rinaldo or Roger Federer. Sad perhaps, but coming from sporting backgrounds we had visions for our son to embrace early morning, evening and weekend training sessions, the camaraderie of a team and to thoroughly enjoy the throes of competition as we had, and as his brothers and sisters had experienced. It would also provide him with the life lessons learned from playing on a team such as giving your all, recovering from failure and the self-discipline necessary to flourish.

As a corporate executive, I had found that many of the recruits I employed who were successful, had been involved in sport at some stage in their lives. These individuals appeared to naturally understand that it took effort, collaboration and grit to succeed. Despite playing and being involved in competition and sport from quite a young age (horse comps at 2!), I was never an all-star athlete. I will say however simply being involved did provide me with a number of these life skills ~ particularly self-discipline. I came to understand that practice made a big difference and it turns out that 'self-discipline is a character trait that engenders *deliberate* practice' [1].

As Professor Anders Ericsson discovered, it's *deliberate* practice that leads to world class performance [2]. *Deliberate* practice is what separates the experts from the average, more so than innate talent or skill [2]. This applies in any domain ranging from music to maths. It is the consistent and deliberate application to improve your performance that creates the expert.

Ericssons' work with psychology professor Angela Duckworth revealed that children who spent time studying in ways they didn't enjoy (independently, repetition, problem solving) performed better than those who *simply* "practiced" [3]. These children were *deliberately* practicing ~ they were improving their performance over time and **that** was their goal and motivation.

Anders Ericssons' Four Essential Components of Deliberate Practice

1. **You must be motivated** to attend to the task and **exert effort to improve your performance**.
2. The design of the task should **take into account your pre-existing knowledge** so that the task can be correctly understood after a brief period of instruction.
3. You should receive **immediate informative feedback** and knowledge of results of your performance.
4. You should **repeatedly perform the same or similar tasks**.

The thing about self-discipline is that it **can** be strengthened; the more you practice it the stronger it becomes. Things like sleep, diet and stress also impact your self-discipline and meditation actually increases it.

Duckworth and Seligman (2005) have found that self-discipline above IQ, is what separates the top students from the average **and** the failure to exercise self-discipline is what causes students to fall short of their intellectual potential. I would say that this is true of life as well, self-discipline is what enables us to reach our potential.

As a parent, I have learned that the one thing that I do genuinely hope for my son is that he enjoys life and is happy ~ if he finds that in sport fantastic; if he doesn't and prefers his other passion of music that's fantastic as well. The bottom line is that it's important to follow your passion, practice it (*deliberately*) and understand that the failures are the real learnings in life, learn from them and carry on.

> "When I was 5 years old, my mother always told me that happiness was the key to life. When I went to school, they asked me what I wanted to be when I grew up. I wrote down 'happy'. They told me I didn't understand the assignment, and I told them they didn't understand life."
>
> *John Lennon*

References

[1] Seligman, Martin. (2011). Flourish: A visionary new understanding of happiness and well-being. Free Press.

[2] Ericsson, K. A. 1. (2016). Peak: Secrets from the new science of expertise. Boston: Houghton Mifflin Harcourt.

[3] Duckworth, Angela. (2016). *Grit: The Power of Passion and Perseverance*. Scribner, New York, NY.

Going Through a Transition? Take Control.

Transitions, whether they be from roles, relationships or through organisational change, offer the individual an opportunity. It is during these times that one has the chance to step back and develop an awareness of one's environment, one's thoughts, feelings and behaviour. Unfortunately, we tend to get caught up in the emotional impact of these transitions and experience negative, ruminating thoughts that neglect to switch off, including feelings of self-doubt and potentially destructive behaviour.

What can you do to manage these inherent negative reactions during times of transition?

You have the control to positively direct your emotions and your behaviour.

Thriving Through Transitions

1. **Breathe** – as simple as it sounds, most of us neglect to take full breaths and experience the benefit of kicking our parasympathetic nervous system (PNS) into action. Our PNS is our "rest and digest" system which is activated by taking deep breaths and exhaling slowly, which in turn activates the vagus nerve. The vagus nerve stimulates the release of acetylcholine (a neurotransmitter) which has a cascade effect throughout the body, promoting an environment of stability and inner-calm.

2. **Stop Multi-tasking** – we spend the majority of our time rushing from activity to activity with our attention under constant demand. Similar to having tabs open in our browsers, our brains also have tabs open, reflecting all of the activities we are meant to be focusing on. Science now tells us that this constant task-switching rapidly depletes our energy stores, leaving us both cognitively and physically exhausted. Our "efficiencies" actually become deficiencies, shown to reduce our productivity by as much as 40%!

3. **Establish a Routine** – when we are going through a transition, it's imperative that we conserve our cognitive energy stores so that we have enough energy to focus on what matters and make the right decisions. Having a morning and evening routine/ritual helps us manage our energy so that we have enough and are ultimately more efficient. Something as simple as selecting your clothes & breakfast the evening before actually reduces your decision making in the morning, keeping your 'tank full' for the important decisions later that day. Something Steve Jobs, Ariana Huffington and Mark Zuckerberg employed early in their careers.

4. **Get Active** – aside from the dopamine release physical activity provides (feel good hormones), increasing blood flow to your brain actually stimulates the production of new brain cells (neurogenesis), reduces and prevents the effects of oxidative stress, and preserves memory stores. [1] Regular physical activity is also an energy booster, fighting fatigue and providing additional energy when you need it most. [2] Don't have the time? Get up 20 minutes earlier and your body & brain will thank-you.

5. **Plan Your Meals** – when going through change, making decisions about what and when to eat are often fraught with desires for quick, readily available, nutrient-poor choices. Researchers have now made a direct link to type of and timing of food and mood, meaning what and how often you eat not only effects your brain's performance, but the thoughts that you have and the feelings that you cultivate.

We're Only Human

We are prone to get 'stuck' in moments and our negativity bias makes it difficult for us to get out.

According to Rick Hanson, author of Hardwiring Happiness, we are essentially suffering from a neuronal hang-over from our prehistoric ancestors, known as our negativity bias. This theory suggests that our sympathetic nervous system is constantly "on" for our survival, keeping our central nervous system in a "fight or flight" state, elevating our cortisol levels (stress hormones) and putting us at risk for mental health issues such as stress, anxiety and depression. As a further consequence, Hanson has discovered that our brains are wired to hold onto the negative emotions (think velcro-like) and seemingly let go of positive emotions (think teflon). The good news is that we can rewire our brains to hold onto the positive and let go of the negative.

Increasing the amount of positive emotions in your life and letting yourself absorb those experiences of positivity can help build neural pathways that combat the negativity bias. Hanson's method suggests you: i) have the experience (or reminisce about a positive experience), ii) enrich it by staying with it for 15 seconds and iii) then absorb it from the top of your head to the tip of your toes. In time you can begin to link these positive emotions/experiences with negative in order to combat the detrimental effects and increase your resilience.

In summary, change and transitions are inevitable, how you manage yourself during these times provides an opportunity to make conscious choices. Build up and absorb positive emotions and apply the 5 strategies above, and you will set yourself up to thrive during these challenging times and throughout life.

References

[1] Davenport, Hogan, Eskes,. Longman, & Poulin (2012). Cerebrovascular Reserve: The Link Between Fitness and Cognitive Function? *Exercise & Sport Sciences Reviews: 40 (3),* 153-158. doi: 10.1097/JES.0b013e3182553430
[2] http://www.webmd.com/diet/news/20061103/exercise-fights-fatigue-boosts-energy

Other

http://www.sciencealert.com/always-switched-on-the-long-term-effects-of-multitasking

https://www.mind.org.uk/information-support/tips-for-everyday-living/
  food-and-mood/
https://www.youtube.com/watch?v=xyQY8a-ng6g
http://www.rickhanson.net/

The Cost of Distraction: How Mindfulness Can Positively Impact Your Bottom Line

"To be mindfully engaged is the most natural, creative
state we can be in".

Ellen Langer

We live in a world where distractions and interruptions are the norm and occur every 3minutes in the typical office environment. What's surprising is that it can take anywhere from 5-23 minutes to re-focus on the task at hand. We may be guilty of spending much too long looking for misplaced files, having an excessive number of tabs open in our browser or perhaps the incessant reminders from our social media lure us in for just one more 'quick check'. These are unconscious activities brought on by mindless behaviour and we tend to operate in this preoccupied, distracted mode every day.

Recent studies indicate that our minds are wandering on average, 46.9% of the time. The unfavourable impact on our focus, productivity, engagement, and interpersonal relationships is far reaching. Gloria Marks has shown that attention distraction can lead to higher stress levels, a negative mood and lower productivity.

According to Medibank Private the Australian economy is losing $34B annually to 'presenteeism' or the loss in productivity when employees come to work yet are not fully productive ~ often due to illness brought on by job stress, lack of work-life balance, unhealthy lifestyle, allergies or illness. Organisations are starting to explore how to address this ever-growing concern and the rise of mindfulness in the workplace has definitely piqued some interest in this regard.

Mindfulness is an awareness that arises through 'paying attention, on purpose, without judgement' (Jon Kabat-Zinn).

If you have the image of yourself sitting in lotus pose (cross legged on the floor), your view of mindfulness is probably limited and there is definitely potential for a broader understanding.

Mindfulness can be practiced anywhere, through almost any activity. Essentially, it involves focusing your attention on whatever it is that you happen to be doing and being immersed in that moment. Concentrated focus on the breath is a common introduction into mindfulness, you may also practice through focusing on what you're eating, focusing on walking, focusing on the body through a body scan and so forth. There are many ways to practice mindfulness and finding one that works for you is important.

So what does all of this 'hippy-like' behaviour do? It literally changes the structure of our brains. In fact, through regular practice, strong evidence demonstrates that it increases the amount of grey matter in the pre-frontal cortex, the anterior cingulate cortex and the hippocampus ~ the areas responsible for things such as attention, decision making, emotion regulation and analytical processing. These areas are also responsible for executive functioning – skills everyone uses to organise and act on information and include: impulse control, flexible thinking, working memory, self monitoring, planning and prioritising. In the latest research, mindful based stress reduction (an 8 week mindfulness program) was **effective for managing work-related stress and boosting psychological resilience in the workplace, particularly when facing stressful situations such as organisational change.**

A daily mindfulness practice has led to a number of positive outcomes across a number of studies and include (but not limited to):

1. Greater clarity and focus [1]
2. Improved self-regulation and overall EQ [2]
3. Enhanced engagement [3]
4. Reduced stress-related illness [4]
5. Improve recall and memory [5]
6. Better sleep [6]
7. Improved immune function [7]

Skeptic or not, mindfulness has evidence-based research behind it, with high impact improvements in overall performance and well-being at work and in life ~ all of which positively impact the bottom line. So ask yourself "why not?" and consider introducing mindfulness into your organisation.

References

[1] Siegel, D. Mindfulness training and neural integration: differentiation of distinct streams of awareness and the cultivation of well-being. Soc Cogn Affect Neurosc (2007) 2 (4): 259-263.

[2] Lykins, E & Baer, R. Psychological Functioning in a Sample of Long-Term Practitioners of Mindfulness Meditation. Jo of Cog Psychotherapy. V23, #3, 2009, 226-241.

[3] Gardner, Frank L., and Zella E. Moore. The psychology of enhancing human performance: The mindfulness-acceptance-commitment (MAC) approach. Springer Publishing Company, 2007.

[4] Grossman, Paul, et al. "Mindfulness-based stress reduction and health benefits: A meta-analysis." Journal of psychosomatic research 57.1 (2004): 35-43.

[5] Zeidan, Fadel, et al. "Mindfulness meditation improves cognition: Evidence of brief mental training." Consciousness and cognition 19.2 (2010): 597-605.

[6] Hülsheger, Alina Feinholdt & Annika Nübold. A low-dose mindfulness intervention and recovery from work: Effects on psychological detachment, sleep quality, and sleep duration Journal of Occupational and Organizational Psychology, Vol

[7] Davidson RJ, Kabat-Zinn J, Schumacher J, Rosenkranz M, Muller D, Santorelli SF, Urbanowski F, Harrington A, Bonus K, Sheridan JF. Alterations in brain and immune function produced by mindfulness meditation. Psychosomatic medicine. 2003 Jul 1;65(4):564-70.

The 3 Things You Should Definitely Do Over the Holidays

It's been one of those years; the final working week is drawing to a close, a welcomed end to the unforgiving pace of 2017. For many of us, the to-do list remains a work-in-progress and our focus is not quite engaged in our plans for next year. "Busy" is the new badge we bear proudly, but is it worth the toll that it's taking on our health? We are physically and cognitively exhausted and addressing *that* exhaustion should be our priority.

1. Reflect

Rather than dwelling on what you *haven't done* this year, start by focusing on all that you *have done*. According to Sue Langley ~ thought leader and leading advisor on practical applications of neuroscience ~ we should all have a "ta-da" list, reminding us of what we've done well each day/month/year. This helps you reflect and increases the likelihood of repeating those positive behaviours. Martin Seligman ~ one of the founders of positive psychology~ recommends a "What Went Well" exercise each day, where you write down what went well that day and why. This simple practice contributes to greater well-being and happiness and decreased symptoms associated with depression. So ask yourself what went well this year and why did it go well?

2. Rest & Restore

Self-compassion is critical at this time of year, the holidays usually unfold at a frenzied pace, laced with expectations to please anyone and everyone. Simply looking after yourself will offer you new-found energy and help you flourish through the next couple of weeks. Aside from routinely getting a good nights sleep, unplug, try meditating for 10 minutes a day, get out in nature and go for long walks. According to Leeds University, spending time in green space has been shown to increase positive emotions, exercise levels and social well-being as well as lowering levels of stress & depression. Exercise of any kind contributes to greater psychological as well as physical well-being.

3. Refocus

Downtime is great but if you're anything like me (Type A, teleologically driven) you prefer to get on top of your goals in order to feel prepared and poised for success. Create positive goals, aligning them with your values and how you want to feel. Begin with mindful journaling where you respond to the prompt: 'by the end of 2018 I.....' and freely write whatever comes to mind (bullet points, sentences, random thoughts). Try mind mapping (great software here to start off with) to marshall your ideas into an organised infographic, offering a mindset of innovation and goal clarity. Danielle LaPorte offers sage advice in creating goals with soul in her book The Desire Map: her key message being to focus on how you want to feel rather than what you want to achieve.

Spend the next few days truly present with your loved ones, rest and have positive foresight for the future. Holidays should always offer some respite from the cut and thrust of a busy existence; enjoy the escape and opportunity to reconnect with yourself.

Set 'Goals with Soul'

With the beginning of the new year upon us, a quick scan through our social media feeds inundates us with advice and wisdom related to the setting resolutions and goals. It all seems too easy, with practical steps to apply in order to increase our chances of following through....so why is it that so many of us fail in doing so?

Behaviour change is simple, but it's not easy.

After only 4 weeks 36% of us have abandoned our resolutions and by the end of the year less than 8% of us actually achieve them. It turns out that the way we have traditionally gone about our goal setting and efforts for breaking or introducing new habits is off-the-mark. Science tells us, there is a better way.

The fact is, resolutions are about behavioural change and involve either adopting new, positive habits or letting go of old, undesirable ones. Our traditional approach has been to address the behaviour, yet what the evidence indicates is that we should be placing our attention on behaviour cues and the subsequent 'rewards' we receive. Let's apply this concept ~ say you'd like to run a marathon...place your running shoes at your bedroom door (cue) so that when you get up, they prompt you to go for a run. Beyond the dopamine 'high' you receive as a reward from the run, reward yourself with a little treat afterwards ~ this may seem counterintuitive but it offers an incentive, further motivating and embedding the behaviour. Over time through repetition the cues will become automatic through the development of neural pathways in the brain ~ essentially you've created a new path to the behaviour or action and that becomes the path of least resistance.

This works in opposition for any habit that you'd like to break.

Aside from focusing on the cue and the reward, there are a number actions that you can employ that will increase the likelihood of sticking to your resolutions & goals and ultimately achieving them.

1. ***Be specific & realistic:*** the more specific and realistic you are, the more likely you are to maintain your resolution. For example, rather than have "lose weight" as a goal, identify how much weight and place a time frame around it. "Lose 15kg by end of Q1." Alternatively if you're unrealistic and place the expectation of say losing 50kg in Q1 you're placing unnecessary stress on yourself along with extremely unrealistic expectations. Consider your resolution a process of constant vigilance rather than a one-off event.

2. ***Identify Steps Required:*** it's important to get specific about what you need to do in order to achieve the goal by creating tasks and milestones. IE. Create a weekly meal plan, limit sugar to so many grams/day, aerobic exercise Mondays, Wednesdays and Fridays at the gym, join a running group for Saturday mornings etc. Then ask yourself what support you will need from your network ~ your partner, your family, your friends, your colleagues. By simply telling other people you have a goal to lose 15kg, you have created an expectation and another degree of accountability.

3. ***Attach meaning & feelings:*** setting goals that are truly meaningful requires breaking them down to your *why* and associating them with how you want to feel. Your why reveals your values behind your goals and operating through your values keeps you focused and intrinsically motivated. When you think about how you want to feel, it offers an emotional conduit and becomes more heart centred rather than just head (ego) centred and often creates positive emotion. When you engage positive emotions (such as gratitude, curiosity, pride, joy, love, inspiration) you broaden your mind and open up to new possibilities and ideas which help build your personal resources (Fredrickson, 2015).

4. ***Employ strategies:*** the fact is you're going to face challenges and potentially experience failure throughout the process, that's life! At the onset acknowledge that you will encounter these challenges and you can either choose to avoid situations where you will be tempted or you can have a strategy to meet that challenge. For ex-

ample, if you're giving up alcohol for 30 days, you can either avoid being in situations where there is alcohol *or* you can plan ahead of time what you will drink when you are in those situations. University professor John Norcross and colleagues found that when individuals preserved their decision making (IE pre-determined a strategy when facing challenges on resolutions), willpower and resolve were stronger.

5. ***Check in with yourself:*** so many of us set our big, hairy, audacious goals at the beginning of the year and neglect to look back at them until the end of the year (if at all). Through the steps and milestones you've created, you can regularly check-in with yourself to make sure you're on track and actioning all of the steps you had originally committed to. On that note, with the challenges comes the occasional slip-up and applying self-compassion is mandatory. If you've missed a week at the gym don't despair! Jump right back up onto that horse and carry-on, don't beat yourself up over it and abandon your goal. After all we're human and bound to crack every now and then.

The good news is that by merely having the intention to change a behaviour or initiate a new one, you're chances of accomplishment are ten-fold (Norcross et al). Once you've identified the core feelings you desire and have subsequently created your goal, truly believe that you can achieve it ~ self-efficacy (belief in your ability to do so) further increases your chances of smashing your goals! Lastly it's essential to think about your daily choices and determine which ones will get you closer to your *why*.

References

Fredrickson, B. (2004). The broaden & build theory of positive emotions. Phil. Trans. Royal Society of London (359), 1367-1377. https://www.ncbi.nlm.nih.gov/pmc/articles/PMC1693418/pdf/15347528.pdf
Laporte, D. (2014). *The Desire Map: A Guide to Creating Goals with Soul*. Sounds True. http://www.daniellelaporte.com/thedesiremap/
https://www.forbes.com/forbes/welcome/?toURL=https://www.forbes.

com/sites/dandiamond/2013/01/01/just-8-of-people-achieve-their-
new-years-resolutions-heres-how-they-did-it/2/&refURL=&referrer
=#752a23b92e2a

http://www.huffingtonpost.com.au/entry/new-years-resolutions-
psychology_us_5862d599e4b0d9a59459654c

http://www.apa.org/monitor/jan04/solutions.aspx

Success Drivers: Motivation

Have you ever sat down to determine what your personal motivators are? Have you considered what it is that drives you? That element that encourages you to set and pursue your goals? How do you stay motivated or keep others motivated ~ particularly when the going gets tough or when your efforts seem fruitless?

Motivation means "to move" and essentially refers to what leads us to take action. Whilst subjective and variable in context, motivation also varies in both nature and focus. What gets *you* out of bed each morning will most likely be different to what gets your partner out of bed, or gets your colleague out of bed and definitely what gets a child out of bed. This drive can change from day-to-day, context-to-context and you have more control over it than you may think.

Researchers have developed a number of theories related to motivation and some interesting conclusions have been drawn. Historically, we have been aligned with intrinsic VS extrinsic sources of motivation. *Intrinsically* we are driven to act for sheer enjoyment and interest whilst *extrinsically* we are moved by an external reward or expectation to meet ~ a clear 'separable outcome'. It turns out that our motivation is much more complex than simply intrinsic/extrinsic factors and our environment along with our social network, play important roles in our decision to take action.

The Evidence

From the dawn of time, we along with our animal counterparts, have done things out of curiosity, adaptiveness and playfulness. Our natural, motivational tendency or our intrinsic drivers were engaged to meet our basic needs. The self-determination theory expands on this to emphasise the influence that our external environment has on our intrinsic needs, particularly our psychological needs of autonomy, competence and relatedness. Social and cultural factors either promote or undermine an individuals 'sense of volition and initiative, in addition to their well-being and the quality of their performance'. Meaning, those we surround ourselves with and our environment ~ both at home and in the workplace, influence our motivation.

The difference in work between someone who offers average performance and someone who goes above and beyond is readily apparent to the most casual observer. One of the expectancy theories has found that the higher the expectations you have for yourself (or for others) the better the corresponding performance. In other words, where you set the bar for yourself (and others) will have a direct impact on the effort you/others exert and on the execution. In some organisations, mediocrity has become acceptable but only because that's where the bar has fallen to and accountability has become a notion of the past. The good news is that by simply raising expectations and moving beyond 'good enough' with modelling of 'what great looks like', behaviours and ultimately cultures can shift. Get out of your comfort zone and strive for things that challenge you.

> Whether you think you can or you can't you're right.
>
> *Henry Ford*

Another theory confirms that if you genuinely believe you have what it takes to accomplish something (self-efficacy), the more effort you'll put in and the more likely you are to achieve your goal. You can increase your self-efficacy through mastery experiences, observing best practice and modelling that behaviour, seeking constructive feedback and lastly through generating physiological states that promote feelings of confidence and minimise anxiety. Organisations can offer talent these types of opportunities through focusing on positive organisational behaviours.

Summary

Whilst our underlying motivations are idiosyncratic and diverse, we now know that we have the capacity to create an environment which bolsters motivation and positively impact effort and performance.

1. Determine how your environment and those in your immediate

circle influence your basic needs. What does that look like for you as an individual and what does it look like for your organisation?

2. Set high expectations for yourself and others, develop stretch goals, create a culture of performance excellence. Step outside of your comfort zone.

3. Increase your self-efficacy and that of others through focusing on positive organisational behaviours (engage mentors, increase opportunity for feedback and implement well-being initiatives).

By employing these practical measures, we can not only increase our motivation, but the motivation and culture within our organisations.

References

https://mmrg.pbworks.com/f/Ryan,+Deci+00.pdf
http://selfdeterminationtheory.org/theory/
http://positivepsychology.org.uk/self-efficacy-definition-bandura-meaning/
http://onlinelibrary.wiley.com/doi/10.1002/job.165/epdf

Success Drivers: Meaning

Organisations, for the most part have come to realise that what talent today really wants more than money or recognition, is meaningful work. Employees want to be a part of the 'bigger picture', they want to contribute their strengths to the greater good, to leave a legacy and to feel passionate towards what they are doing each and every day. What makes this challenging is that we all view meaning through different lenses, we have different values and at least 2/3 of us aren't aware of our core strengths. Furthermore, each generation defines meaningful work differently. It's difficult to become a part of the 'bigger picture' if we don't even have a foundation or a framework from which to draw.

Many of us are on a journey to the self, an exploration into who we truly are, what we truly want, where we want to be and how we want to be spending our time. On the one hand, it can be challenging to do this within the confines of an organisation and on the other, there are some organisations who encourage this self-discovery; the latter being the preferred employers of choice. Regardless, it is up to the individual to drive this journey and there are a few things that you can do to make a start.

Journey to Self

1. Complete a values exercise and determine what your core values are. We generally know what's important to us, actually taking the time to identify values and understand what they actually mean to us is another story. Knowing what your values are increases your focus, improves your clarity, helps you make decisions and drives your motivation. [1]

2. Complete a strengths assessment. We typically think we know what our strengths are, but have you ever completed an assessment to put names to them and develop a language surrounding what you enjoy doing and what gives you energy? People who know and use their strengths are happier, more engaged and more likely to achieve their goals. [2]

3. Draft up a job description of your ideal job including day-to-day responsibilities and tasks. How would your strengths be operationalised through your dream role?

4. Reflecting on your dream job, are there any competencies required that you don't possess or perhaps need to improve? Consider if this requires further on-the-job experience **or** if there are external options for developing these skills further.

5. What activities do you currently find meaning from? What lights your fire, strengthens your resolve and encourages you to get out of bed each day? Can you do more of it? According to Sonja Lyubomirsky 40% of our happiness lies in our intentional activities, the more we choose happiness, the happier we become. [3]

6. Working with a mentor/coach has been extremely helpful for me on my own journey, particularly someone who challenges me and holds me accountable. Someone who holds up the mirror to remind me that I'm on the right path, that good things are on the horizon because of my actions and I am doing what I love, working with people that I like, under my terms. Essentially having a mentor/coach guides you on your journey and corrects you when you go off-course.

It's a long journey, but boy am I glad I started it.

References

[1] https://www.huffingtonpost.com/karen-naumann/feeling-stuck-5-reasons-why-values-matter_b_9075222.html
[2] https://www.strengthsprofile.com/
[3] https://www.psychologytoday.com/blog/one-among-many/201503/happy-pie

PART 3: WELL-BEING

An elusive construct often confused with 'wellness', well-being is beyond physical health and vitality. Occasionally interchanged with happiness (to Martin Seligman's dismay), well-being is about cultivating, possessing and harnessing the personal resources to meet the challenges life throws your way. It's multi-faceted through psychological, social and physical means. Well-being leads to flourishing and the ability to rise to the occasion, whatever the circumstances are. Well-being incorporates self-care, self-compassion and discipline; it manifests through positive emotion, engagement, positive relationships, meaning and achievement. Equipping yourself with the tools and competencies you need for the nuances of leadership and life lie at the foundation of well-being.

The Road to Well-being at Work

Top organisations regard their people as their most important asset, and accordingly these organisations consistently invest in employee well-being. Well-being is no longer merely a nice to have, it's a must have. When companies support and promote well-being employees become happier, healthier and more productive. Every dollar invested receives an average of $5 returned (Rath & Harter, 2010) and upwards of $9. This return is demonstrated through increases in productivity, improvements in customer relations and overall cost savings (see WOW business case). What's even more compelling is that it can be measured, and measured recurrently to monitor the effects of the various programs implemented.

Well-being has been positively correlated with increases in engagement, life and job satisfaction, happiness, motivation, energy, health, collaboration and more (see WOW Site). But as an organisation, where do you start?

Initially, it's imperative that well-being is defined within the organisation; what does it represent at an individual level and broadly speaking, an organisational level? To date, there are a number of constructs and descriptions of individual well-being however, very few empirical definitions. In 2012, researchers provided a simple, clear cut definition (and diagram below) backed by substantial evidence: 'well-being is a balance point between an individuals resource pool and the challenges they face' (Dodge, Daly, Huyton & Sanders, 2012).

Psychological, social and physical components are all aspects of well-being, it's up to the organisation to determine which element to address first.

Starting with **psychological**, consider the fact that depression is the leading cause of disability worldwide (WHO, 2016). The state of Australia's mental health reveals that 1/5 Australians between 18-65 will deal with a mental health issue within the next 12 months, and 45% of Australians will experience a mental health issue over the course of their lifetime (ABS, 2007). 85% of Australian workers will experience stress leading to over 20 million sick days each year (Medibank Private 2014). Tally this up with the cost to the Australian economy at $14.8 billion and to the companies at $10.1 billion (Medibank Private, 2008) and our case for well-being becomes even more compelling.

There are many, many approaches an organisation can take to support **psychological well-being**. The positive psychology literature is ripe with constructs and theories to spearhead a highly impactful program. Don't have the time to drudge through the past 15+ years of literature? Hire a professional/consultant to create and launch your well-being mission (click here). The benefits of elevating psychological well-being are vast and include things such as improved EQ, overall happiness, strengthened interpersonal relationships, heightened creativity, improved coping and less stress. Some of the research:

- Ryff's model of psychological well-being leading to optimal psychological functioning, consists of six domains: establishment of quality ties to other, pursuit of meaningful goals, ability to manage complex environments, continued growth and development, sense of autonomy in thought and self acceptance (Ryff & Keyes, 1995)

- Seligman's Well-Being theory PERMA suggests these 5 areas that lead to flourishing/psychological well-being: positive emotion, engagement, positive relationships, meaning/purpose and accomplishment (Seligman, 2012).

- Mental health is defined by the WHO (2016) a state of well-being in which every individual realises his or her own potential, can cope with the normal stresses of life, can work productively and fruit-fully, and is able to make a contribution to her or his community

Social efforts across organisations have been on the rise. It was traditionally thought that 'work' and 'life' were best kept as two separate entities however, with the technological boom and latest findings in psychology and neuroscience, organisations are discovering the benefit of integrating and supporting social well-being. Similar to psychological well-being, there are a number of theories and constructs out there that are sometimes difficult to decipher. Let's highlight a few of the key findings and take-aways.

- Theoretically substantiated are the five components of social well-being presented by Keyes (1998): social integration, social contribution, social coherence, social actualisation and social acceptance. Explore ways to incorporate these into your social well-being approach.

- Emma Seppala reports that having high social connections provides greater psychological well-being, improvements in physical health and immune function in contrast to low social connection which is actually worse than smoking, obesity and high blood pressure (House, Landis & Umberson, 1988). (note: quality of connections vs quantity)

- People who feel more connected to others have less risk of anxiety and depression (Lee, Draper & Lee, 2001)

- Rillings et al (2002) discovered that social cooperation activates our rewards circuitry in the brain which reinforces positive choices in helping

- Work groups and manager-employee relations can be defined as autonomy-controlling or autonomy supportive, the latter of which leads to higher job satisfaction, trust and collaboration (Deci et al, 1989)

Developing a social well-being agenda is a game changer for any organisation, again there are many ways to do this, engage a professional and be sure to measure the impact.

Physical well-being has definitely been the most prominent resource organisations have focused on in recent years. Vitality programs, wellness programs, wearables and the like have become ingrained in corporate culture. For the most part, organisations who are doing this are doing it well. Where a few organisations are falling short is quite often in leading from the top-down. Despite providing opportunities for employee well-being our corporate leaders are not necessarily participating in these opportunities themselves, even though they are the ones who likely need it most. Of note, leaving the choice to employees is key ~ not everyone likes to mix their fitness regime within the working environment. The benefits of physical well-being are widely known. In the workplace improvements in physical well-being have been linked to increases in employee engagement, creativity, innovation and productivity +++ (Australian Government, Comcare 2011). So again, compelling evidence to implement a physical well-being/wellness program if you have yet to do so!

All programs (psychological, social, physical) should be evidence based, appeal to the masses and definitely be sustainable. Furthermore, you certainly want to assess and measure the impact of the program against engagement and the bottom line, as well as the influence it has on subjective, individual and work-related well-being. Many of these tools come at little or no cost depending on how streamlined and automatic you want the processes and the report(s). Lastly, ensure you are driving this from both top-down and bottom-up. There's nothing worse then getting the keys to a Ferrari but not having enough money to fill it with petrol. Invest the capital and the manpower and your returns will be prolific.

References

Australian Bureau of Statistics, (2007). National Survey of Mental Health and Wellbeing: Summary of Results, Table 1.

Deci, E. L., Connell, J.E. & Ryan, R.M. (1989). Self determination in a work organization. *Journal of Applied Psychology,* 74(4), 580-590.

Dodge, R., Daly, A., Huyton, J., & Sanders, L. (2012). The challenge of defining wellbeing. *International Journal of Wellbeing*, 2(3), 222-235. doi:10.5502/ijw.v2i3.4

House, J., Landis, K. & Umberson, D. (1988). Social relationships and health. *Science*241(4865): 540-545.

Keyes CLM. Social well-being. *Social Psychology Quarterly*. 1998;61:121–140.

Lee, R., Draper, M. & Lee, S. () Social connectedness: dysfunctional interpersonal behaviours and psychological distress: Testing a mediator model. *Journal of Counselling Psychology*, 48(3): 310-318.

Page, K.M. & Vella-Brodrick, D.A. (2009). The what, why and how of employee wellbeingL a new model. *Social Indicators Research Journal*, 90: 441.

Rillings, J., Gutman, D., Zeh, T., Pagoni, G., Berns, G. & Kilts, C. A neural basis for social cooperation. *Neuron,* 2002 Jul 18;35(2):395-405 doi: http://www.sciencedirect.com/science/article/pii/S0896627302007559

Ryff, C. & Keyes, C. (1995). The structure of psychological well-being revisited. *Journal of Personality and Social Psychology*, 69(4): 719-727.

Seligman, M. E. (2012). *Flourish: A visionary new understanding of happiness and well-being.* Simon and Schuster.

World Health Organization (2016). Out of the Shadows: Making Mental Health a Global Development Priority. Washington, DC.

Human Doing VS Human Being

Life is busy. We are inundated with apps, email, to-do lists, projects, family responsibilities and all that life throws our way. We are stretched, relentlessly tired and often find ourselves "personally and professionally depleted". [1] Our boundaries are crossed, our down-time is non-existent and if we could just outsource a few things to help us get on top of it all, we could breathe. So why don't we?

Too often we put everyone else's priorities and feelings first when what we really need to be doing is looking after number one.

We've become so ingrained in human 'doing' that we are neglecting human 'being' and ultimately neglecting ourselves. Expectations (societal, others & our own) along with our egos prevent us from seeking help, from taking a break, from replenishing our resources. The best thing you can do for yourself is put your ego and those expectations aside and take stock. Strive for authenticity and meaning....be mindful of your actions.

"Expectation is the root of all heartache."

Shakespeare

What Can You Do Today?

1. **Reflect** ~ Write everything down that's taking up space in your brain. Your brain is similar to your computer: the more tabs you have open in your browser, the less efficient your computer is. The same thing goes for your brain and all of the things you have on your mind ~ they are sapping you of your energy and creativity. What's working for you? Are you aligned with your priorities? Be kind to yourself, avoid ruminating thoughts and worry, reframe the way you perceive stress.

2. **Recover** ~ Nourish your mind, body and spirit. Allow yourself to daydream, invite stillness into your life and take care of your phys-

iological needs (sleep, eat a brain-healthy diet and exercise). Spend time with family and friends, escape the day-to-day, get into green space, unplug.

3. **Reset** ~ Create a plan for the next 6 months, one that's flexible and agile enough to account for lifes' curve balls. Instil practical, daily rituals that support you on all fronts (particularly morning rituals). When something attempts to derail your focus ask yourself "is this going to contribute to me achieving my goals?"...if not, let it go. Practice kaizen.

Our self-care is critical to our performance and overall wellbeing. The more compassion we have for ourselves, the more we are able to foster a growth mindset that views obstacles as opportunities and failure as a necessary component of success. The more compassion we have for ourselves, the more potential we have to thrive and set a positive example for others. When was the last time you checked in on yourself?

References

[1] Gelles, David. (2015). Mindful Work. Profile Books Ltd. London.

Other

https://www.brainpickings.org/2015/01/26/anne-lamott-stitches-hope-1/
https://www.bbcgoodfood.com/howto/guide/10-foods-boost-your-brainpower
https://qz.com/804022/health-benefits-japanese-forest-bathing/
http://www.becomingminimalist.com/unplug-please/
https://www.inc.com/quora/why-your-morning-ritual-is-so-important-to-your-success.html

Proactively Prepare for Stress

As a country we are riddled with anxiety. 2 million Australians suffer from this mental health condition and Beyondblue reports that 20% of those with chronic anxiety wait as long as six years before seeking help (!). Part of the problem (of not seeking help) rests with the stigma of admitting you are not ok whilst the other part is driven by your own self-talk.

The coping mechanisms sought out to manage stress and ultimately anxiety end up being in the form of drugs, alcohol or self-defeating behaviours. Cue the self-talk which offers little comfort to the sufferer. On the contrary there is an inclination to berate yourself for the lack of willpower, self-regulation and competence. This can lead to a vicious cycle which often results in more 'coping', more negative self-talk and consequently more anxiety.

Let's face it, we all experience anxiety from time to time and like stress, in certain doses it can be a motivator. However, for those with chronic anxiety the rumination (overthinking) and negative self-talk does not stop. And when we do finally seek help, we are so far down the path that it ends up being in the form of a pharmaceutical (Xanax or Valium being the leading remedies). And that's ok! Sometimes we need a bridge to help us across to the other side of whatever it is that we're dealing with, the important part being that help has been actively sought.

Equipping Yourself for Stress

There are measures we can take ahead of time, even when we're feeling on top of our game, that can help us deal with anxiety and not only cope during those times of stress, but thrive.

1. The first thing is to **become aware** of how you're feeling early on and this can be accomplished through meditation. The evidence behind a regular meditation practice is growing exponentially and one of its' key contributions is increasing our self-awareness. When we're always "on" and rushing from place-to-place

task-to – task, we often neglect ourselves and become oblivious to how we are truly feeling. It's the "I don't have time for myself" mentality when the reality is you must make time for yourself. By increasing your self-awareness, you start to listen to that negative chatter going on in your mind, you start to notice how your body is responding to stress and you start taking measures to recalibrate.

2. The next thing to employ is **self-compassion**. We so often put ourselves last on our priority list that when we realise we aren't coping and are feeling the physical consequences of our lifestyle, we've reached the point of burning out. We've hit a wall and recovering becomes a serious challenge so rather than recover we self-medicate. Being kind to yourself begins with addressing that little voice in your head that pushes you beyond your limits and changing what that voice is saying. Through practicing self-compassion, your inside voice becomes positive and you begin making time for yourself and filling your resource bucket.

3. Adopting a regular **exercise** routine is one of the best antidotes for stress and anxiety. Not only does it help you recover from stressful experiences faster physically, but it prepares you both physically and mentally for dealing with those situations so that you approach them from a balanced perspective. Physical training in the morning prepares your brain for the day and enables you to approach challenges less reactively and with a clear head.

4. What's in your pantry also influences how you manage stress. Despite being only 3% of our body weight our brain consumes 20% of the energy we intake, **fueling it appropriately** is key to managing stress and anxiety. Transfats (in the form of pies, margarine, frozen pizzas, pastries etc) wreak havoc on our brains decision making and problem solving abilities. They also contribute to sluggish thinking and prevent the production of serotonin (happiness hormone) and Omega-3 (essential for brain function). Studies have linked this to poor brain performance and even depression. A med-

iterranean diet has been shown to improve brain performance and protects the brain from future ailments.

5. Psychologist Kelly McGonigals' groundbreaking work on **reframing stress** recommends you adjust the way you respond to stress. The four steps above can help you do this, along with employing curiosity ie: asking 'will this matter in five years?' or 'in the scheme of things is this so bad?' or through simply taking a deep breath. Deep breathing activates the parasympathetic nervous system (in as little as 6 seconds) which signals our relaxation response, slowing our heart rate, reducing the release of stress hormones (cortisol) and instigating the release of calming hormones (oxytocin) throughout our brain and body.

"Stress is not the problem, its the lack of recovery".

Tal Ben-Shahar

Instilling the above practices into your life are a sure-fire way to increase the resources you have available to you so that you can not only function through periods of stress but flourish.

References

https://www.facebook.com/beyondblue/
https://health.clevelandclinic.org/2015/07/avoid-these-10-foods-full-of-trans-fats/
https://www.psychologytoday.com/blog/the-resilient-brain/201506/trans-fats-bad-your-brain
https://www.nbcnews.com/health/health-news/mediterranean-diet-could-save-your-brain-study-finds-n703216

Hardwiring Your Brain for Well-Being

You've just done something really well....nailed a presentation, delivered the consummate performance, won a case, completed a successful operation. Everyone in the room is telling you that you did a great job, they loved it, high-fives all around etc. However, there is that **one** person who offers something negative. Thereafter the negative sticks with you, the positive has sifted through.

The reality is our brains are hardwired this way ~ we are prone to hold onto negative experiences (and build corresponding negative neural pathways) all the while failing to pay sufficient attention to the positive; historically, this was potentially the difference between dying and surviving. A type of neuronal hangover you might say.

We can even become our *own* harshest critics through our individual negativity bias. The good news is that we can change the inclination to hold onto the negative, and we are also able to overcome our negativity bias so that we refrain from having those negative thoughts or offering those negative comments.

> "Your brain has a hair-trigger readiness to go negative
> to help you survive."
>
> *Rick Hanson*

Neuropsychologist and professor Rick Hanson has demonstrated that by having or even reminiscing about positive experiences, enriching those experiences by staying with them for 12 seconds and then 'absorbing' those experiences through visualisation ~ it is possible to build positive neural pathways. Hanson's book Hardwiring Happiness explores this in great detail and he calls this exercise 'taking in the good'.

The conversion of positive mental states to lasting neural traits requires effort since we are consistently working against our negativity bias. Hanson and others have identified a ratio for positive to negative emotions: for each negative emotion you need three-five positive emotions to balance this out; in the workplace it's five and in relationships it's as high as seven! (Fredrickson, 2012; Hanson, 2015).

> "Our negativity bias creates an ongoing vulnerability to stress, anxiety, disappointment and hurt."
>
> *Rick Hanson*

Our brains operating systems have two settings: responsive and reactive. In our responsive state, we rise to challenges, are un-phased by stressors and comfortably deal with threats, loss and rejection without getting caught up in the emotions and unhealthy behavioural patterns. We feel safe, satisfied and connected with others. Our parasympathetic nervous system is active, leading to the release of feel-good hormones, slowing our heart rate and lowering our blood pressure.

Then there is our reactive mode: the mode that evolved through our ancestors to help keep them safe when disturbed by threat (think lions, starvation and foe). The reactive mode disturbs the calming effect of the responsive mode, activates our sympathetic nervous system (fight or flight centre), fires up our amygdala and releases stress hormones. This reactive mode that kept our ancestors alive lights up when our autonomy is threatened, when we are worried about money, feeling pressured at work or experiencing social pain. Toggling between the two modes is typical, yet occasionally we can get caught up in the reactive mode, neglecting the need for recovery.

Over time our reactive system can place us into a state of sympathetic nervous system dominance which is similar to pouring battery acid on our brains (specifically the hippocampus responsible for memory and learning). Practices like 'taking in the good' and meditation can cultivate an environment in the brain and body for being more responsive.

By 'taking in the good' and/or meditating, a space is created between the stimulus of stress and our response to that stimulus. An individual can also equip themselves with positive mental and psychological resources that will contribute to their overall well-being. So try it now... think of a moment that put a smile on your face recently, enrich it by staying with those feelings for 12 seconds.....and feel your body absorb those feelings from the top of your head to the tip of your toes.

That's it, that really **is** all there is to it. Next try it in the moment and over time you will find that you become more present in every moment, leading to you becoming a happier, more engaged, more resilient individual.

To take the positivity test go to: http://www.positivityratio.com/single.php.

For more information and resources from Rick Hanson visit his website here: http://www.rickhanson.net/

Thanks to Rick Hanson for his wonderful book & practical insights into our ever-evolving brain!

References

Fredrickson, Barbara. (2012). Positivity : Groundbreaking Research to Release Your Inner Optimist and Thrive. OneWorld Publications, London, UK.
Hanson, Rick. (2015). Hardwiring Happiness : How to reshape your brain and your life. Ebury Publishing, London, UK.

Social Well-Being: Human Connection Matters

"Other people matter."

Christopher Peterson

Human connection matters. It not only makes us happier and less stressed but also creates an environment that contributes to us living longer.

In one of Harvard's longest standing longitudinal studies (spanning 80 years+), researchers found that: *"close relationships, more than money or fame, are what keep people happy throughout their lives.... Those ties protect people from life's discontents, help to delay mental and physical decline, and are better predictors of long and happy lives than social class, IQ, or even genes."*

Unfortunately, we live in a time where there is an erosion of empathy and compassion (Goleman, 2013). We are an over-worked, over-stressed, overwhelmed society drawn to the incessant lure of technology; the negative impact on our presence and relationships is far-reaching.

Despite being 'hardwired to connect' as Matthew Lieberman explains in his book Social, our hardwiring also predisposes us to initially move away from others when we first meet or when we are placed into a new social situation. Why does this happen? According to neuroscientist Evian Gordon we have a minimise danger, maximise reward network which prompts us to move towards rewards and away from threats. On top of this network, our negativity bias kicks in and responds to new situations/people as threatening.

This constant vigilance is taxing on our sympathetic nervous system (SNS) placing us into SNS dominance. SNS dominance leads to a steady release of cortisol (and other stress hormones), which in the long-term can damage our hippocampus (area in the brain for spatial memory and learning) and lead to stress-induced illness. It can also lead to a significant decrease in our productivity.

Social well-being is a differentiator for organisations. It has been linked with improvements in engagement, productivity and overall well-being. What are a few things leaders & organisations can do to elevate social well-being?

1. Encourage social contribution (IE. volunteer days, community projects and workplace giving).
2. Create common goals for teams to strive for with underlying core company values (social integration and coherence).
3. Promote social acceptance (tolerance of differences and diversity).
4. Create opportunities for team bonding (something fun!)
5. Establish a mentorship program

Gallup polled 15 million workers and found that individuals are 7x as likely to be engaged in their work if they had high quality friendships on the job.

Furthermore, leaders who demonstrate empathy and compassion raise the degree of social well-being across the entire organisation. People need to feel they are understood, appreciated and accepted. Empathy and compassion satisfy each of these needs.

But what can you do as an individual to positively engage with others?

1. Limit your technology & social media (put rituals in place to break the bad habit).
2. Meditate (increasing your focus will increase your presence).
3. Savour your positive experiences (happier people make better connections with others).

Our brains are social organs, they thrive on human connection. Understanding how to link social well-being with organisational imperatives is key to the sustainability and performance of any organisation. It's also the key to personal fulfilment and happiness.

References

https://news.harvard.edu/gazette/story/2017/04/over-nearly-80-years-
    harvard-study-has-been-showing-how-to-live-a-healthy-and-
    happy-life/
https://www.youtube.com/watch?v=HTfYv3IEOqM
https://www.youtube.com/watch?v=NNhk3owF7RQ
https://www.strategy-business.com/article/09306
https://siyli.org/resources/quality-relationships-the-foundation-of-health

Daydream Believers: The Unfocused Mind

As a mindfulness practitioner and performance consultant, I have found that one of the primary drivers for leaders initiating mindfulness programs within their organisation is to enhance focus. Imagine their surprise when I correspondingly emphasise the importance of not focusing.

Not focusing activates the brains default mode network (DMN) creating an environment in the brain that fosters creativity, increases self-awareness, hardwires long-term memory and improves decision making. (Baird et al, 2012; Smallwood et al, 2009; Bergland, 2013; Pillay, 2017).

It turns out that focusing too much exhausts our prefrontal cortex (PFC) known as the executive centre of the brain. Aside from focus, the PFC is also responsible for rational thinking, emotion regulation, decision making, emotional intelligence and impulse control. Learning how to manage your energy in this area of the brain not only improves its performance but also the efficiency at which it operates.

The costs associated with daydreaming (on our productivity, relationships, attention) can often outweigh the benefits however, understanding how to take advantage of this natural process so that it becomes an advantage, is a skill that can be developed. (McMillan et al, 2013).

As a whole we spend almost half of our days lost in thought, constantly task switching as distractions emerge persistently vying for our attention. It's not all bad news however, we can take advantage of this time by consciously stimulating the DMN. According to Srini Pillay in his recent article in HBR (May 2017), we can intentionally activate the DMN through three pathways: positive constructive daydreaming (PCD), napping and actually pretending to be someone else when problem solving.

Here's How:

1) PCD can be deliberately built into your day whilst you are performing a low-key activity (making coffee, reading the paper, washing the dishes). Essentially any task that is low demanding can enable you to explore the nooks and crannies of your mind and tap into your imagination. It consists of stimulating playful, wishful imagery and planful, creative thought (Singer, 1974).

2) Napping for as little as 10minutes has been shown to raise clarity and attentiveness. IF you're *really* looking to bolster creativity you'll need a solid 90 minutes however, longer naps have also been linked to grogginess on waking.

3) "Psychological Halloween" according to Pillay suggests a type of role-playing where you pretend to be someone else whilst problem solving. It enables you to get out of your own mindset and step into someone else's. It also encourages you to let go of both your conscious and unconscious bias. The six hats approach to problem solving takes advantage of a similar concept.

Practicing mindfulness may compliment each of these practices and possibly expedite access to the DMN. Social psychologist and Harvard University professor Ellen Langer explains mindfulness as letting go of preconceived notions and viewing experiences with child-like curiosity; it incorporates changing your mindset and supports Pillays' notion of behaving as someone else with fresh eyes.

Begin organising your days so that you take advantage of structured periods of focus (IE 90 minute blocks to "get shit done") as well as periods of being unfocused. Toggling between the two will help you manage your energy, raise your performance and get those creative juices flowing.

References

Baird B., Smallwood J., Mrazek M.D., Kam J.W., Franklin M.S., & Schooler J.W. (2012). Inspired by distraction: mind wandering facilitates creative incubation. *Psychological Science,* Oct 1; 23(10):1117-22.

Singer, J.L. (1974). Daydreaming and the stream of thought. *American Science*, Jul-Aug; 62(4):417-25.

Smallwood, J., Nind, L. & O'Connor R.C. (2009). When is your head at? An exploration of the factors associated with the temporal focus of the wandering mind. *Conscious Cognition*, Mar; 18(1):118-25.

http://blog.iqmatrix.com/six-thinking-hats

https://www.forbes.com/sites/daviddisalvo/2012/07/24/why-you-should-take-a-10-minute-nap-every-day/#cb3e5921b0f5

https://hbr.org/2017/05/your-brain-can-only-take-so-much-focus

Mental Training: Your Secret Weapon

Surprisingly it only takes a few minutes a day to harness your mind and shape your brain in order to increase your performance. But why doesn't everyone do it? For some the simplicity of the action undermines the actual benefit, for others it's yet another item to place on their never-ending 'to-do' list, and for most, uncertainty around where to start prevents them from starting at all.

Fortunately, there are a variety of practices that you can undertake which will not only enhance your performance, but also help you manage stress and increase your overall well-being.

Mental Training Practices

1. **Visualisation**
2. **Meditation**
3. **Taking in the Good**
4. **Gratitude**
5. **Positive Emotions**

VISUALISATION When asked about perfecting his stroke, Michael Phelps shares that he repeatedly visualises each movement and turn he executes through the water the night prior to each race. In fact top athletes across most sports have long prescribed to the notion that visualisation supports them in their pursuit of excellence. Interestingly, professor of Neurology at Harvard University Alvero Pascual-Leone has discovered that merely visualising an action contributes to building the brain circuitry responsible for performing that action ~ in particular it resembles the neuroplasticity of actually practicing the action. Meaning that repeatedly visualising your performance literally develops the brain pathways required to perform.

MEDITATION Prior to taking the stage at any event, Steve Jobs would spend a few moments in meditation. He did this in order to manage stress, increase his engagement with the audience and ground himself in the present moment. Regular mindful meditation practice strengthens the prefrontal cortex (PFC) ~ the executive centre of our brain responsible for focus, judgement, planning, decision making, impulse control etc. When we experience stress, the chemicals produced (cortisol) notify our amygdala in our brain (our fight or flight centre) and essentially act as a roadblock to the operations of the PFC. Strengthening the PFC through meditation allows you to retain control of this centre and mitigate and manage the negative effects of stress. Meditation also provides you with exceptional awareness to the extent that you become in tune to others emotions, elevating your empathy and improving your interpersonal relationships.

TAKING IN THE GOOD Thanks to our ancestors we are hardwired to react negatively to stressful situations in order to survive. Unfortunately this has resulted in a negativity bias meaning that our brain automatically reverts to negative and holds onto negative experiences much longer than positive. Rick Hanson has discovered that by having (or reminiscing about) positive experiences, we can combat the inclination to become immersed in the negative. Further enriching positive experiences by staying with them and then 'absorbing them' through visualisation (top of our heads to tip of our toes) – enables us to hardwire ourselves for happiness. Additional benefits of this process relate to our stress response. As mentioned above, when we are stressed our body releases cortisol which kills cells in our hippocampus – the area responsible for visuo-spatial memory and also responsible for calming the amygdala down. When we regularly take in the good, we change our response to stress, less cortisol is released and our hippocampus remains unharmed.

GRATITUDE The evidence behind gratitude indicates that a regular practice (once a week is more beneficial than daily!) contributes to our overall happiness and life satisfaction. Gratitude also improves physical and psychological health, relationships and sleep. Each of the benefits of gratitude positively impact performance and engagement, so taking the time once a week to express 5 things you are grateful for is definitely worth the effort!

POSITIVE EMOTION Positive emotions have the ability to provide an upward spiral towards not only happiness, but also resilience, physical health and overall well-being. Furthermore Barbara Fredrickson and Marcel Losada have found that in order to flourish in life we need to be experiencing 3 positive emotions to each negative ~known as the positivity ratio. Which positive emotions are most beneficial? Fredrickson has created a top 10: *pride, interest, gratitude, curiosity, serenity, hope, amusement, inspiration, awe* and *love*. Seek out opportunities for these emotions and utilise these emotions in your mindset.

If we all put as much time into developing our mental capacities as we did worrying about the future or ruminating about the past, what a richer place our minds would be. It really is as simple as I've explained above, take a few moments each day and take advantage of your not-so-secret weapon.

References

https://www.psychologytoday.com/blog/the-athletes-way/201312/how-does-daydreaming-help-form-long-lasting-memories

http://www.amenclinics.com/blog/what-is-the-executive-center-of-the-brain/

http://www.rickhanson.net/

http://greatergood.berkeley.edu/article/item/are_you_getting_enough_positivity_in_your_diet

https://greatergood.berkeley.edu/article/item/why_gratitude_is_good

https://www.forbes.com/sites/amymorin/2014/11/23/7-scientifically-proven-benefits-of-gratitude-that-will-motivate-you-to-give-thanks-year-round/#a39b5f9183c0

Harnessing Stress for Good

85% of Australians will experience stress on the job within the next twelve months, resulting in 20 MILLION sick days. This will cost the Australian economy and private companies nearly $25 BILLION collectively. In the U.S it's estimated at $300 BILLION. In One Year.

It's small wonder that organisations are investing substantially in well-being programs and promoting wellness initiatives. Worthy long term enterprise indeed but is there something that you can do now to support yourself when its needed most?

"Your perception of stress influences your body's response to stress."
Kelly McGonigal

Knowing that stressful occurrences are inevitably a part of your future, there are a number of measures you can take to not only cope but also prosper through these experiences (many of which were discussed in my previous article on how to Proactively Prepare for Stress). It turns out that by also adjusting your stress mindset (or your perception of stress) you can positively influence your ability to manage your stress response.

According to health psychologist and lecturer from Stanford University Kelly McGonigal, stress is not the problem, it's our perception of stress that can lead to a poor mind-body response. This notion is supported by previous work suggesting that it is our cognitive appraisal of stress that determines whether it is harmful and how we will respond to it.

Think about your parents and how they perceive stressors in their lives.... chances are it's quite different to how you may perceive life stressors. Think about your spouse, your siblings, your best mate.... it's also likely that they too perceive stressors in their lives differently. The reality is, some of us thrive during times of stress, rising to the challenge, excited and motivated whereas others resort to fight or flight, feelings of helplessness and inaction. Some of us have a negative stress response to a particular situation whereas some of us flourish under the same circumstances. Why is this the case? The short answer is that we all perceive stress differently.

According to McGonigal, there are 3 protective beliefs that influence our perception and response to stressors:

1. Your bodies response to stress is helpful.
2. You are able to handle and even learn and grow from the stress in your life.
3. Stress as something that everyone deals with.

In order to interpret your initial stress response as a signal of meaning rather than of inadequacy, McGonigal says that you need courage and self-compassion.

Possessing high self-efficacy (the belief in your ability to meet the challenges you face) creates a platform for courage. When you first experience a situation that activates your stress response, cultivate the belief that it is possible to transform the stress into a positive rather than interpret it as purely negative. View stress as an opportunity to learn and grow. Take a deep breath to initiate your relaxation response which floods your body with acetylcholine, dopamine and other neurotransmitters that emit a calming effect, counteracting the stress hormones (cortisol and adrenalin) that your stress response elicited. Next, avoid listening to your inner critic that is often triggered with your stress response and instead genuinely believe in your ability to cope and prosper. Be kind to yourself.

The latest evidence indicates that not having any stress in your life is worse for your health than having stress in your life and managing it well. Stress can encourage us to reach out to others, help us overcome obstacles and motivate us to achieve our goals. In fact, researchers have determined that having a positive mindset towards stress can lead us to a more optimistic outlook, increase our drive and compassion and even boost our productivity at work!

So, I suppose you could say that stress has been given a bad rap. You now have the opportunity to harness the energy that stress generates and make use of the cleverness of your body's initial stress response. Make stress the stimulus for your initiative, effort and discipline, enable it to be a force for good.

References

McGonigal, Kelly. (2016). *The Upside of Stress.* Penguin Random House, NY, NY.
https://link.springer.com/
referenceworkentry/10.1007%2F978-1-4419-1005-9_1115